The Cost of a Military Person-Year

A Method for Computing Savings from Force Reductions

Carl J. Dahlman

Prepared for the Office of the Secretary of Defense
Approved for public release; distribution unlimited

RAND NATIONAL DEFENSE RESEARCH INSTITUTE

The research described in this report was prepared for the Office of the Secretary of Defense (OSD). The research was conducted in the RAND National Defense Research Institute, a federally funded research and development center sponsored by the OSD, the Joint Staff, the Unified Combatant Commands, the Department of the Navy, the Marine Corps, the defense agencies, and the defense Intelligence Community under Contract W74V8H-06-C-0002.

Library of Congress Cataloging-in-Publication Data

Dahlman, Carl J., 1950–
The cost of a military person-year : a method for computing savings from force reductions / Carl J. Dahlman.
p. cm.
Includes bibliographical references.
ISBN 978-0-8330-4151-7 (pbk. : alk. paper)
1. United States—Armed Forces—Pay, allowances, etc. I. Title.

UC74.D34 2007
355.6'223—dc22

2007027911

Published 2007 by the RAND Corporation
1776 Main Street, P.O. Box 2138, Santa Monica, CA 90407-2138
1200 South Hayes Street, Arlington, VA 22202-5050
4570 Fifth Avenue, Suite 600, Pittsburgh, PA 15213-2665
RAND URL: http://www.rand.org/
To order RAND documents or to obtain additional information, contact
Distribution Services: Telephone: (310) 451-7002;
Fax: (310) 451-6915; Email: order@rand.org

Preface

The study documented in this book aims at constructing a better analytical foundation for the costing of military personnel for use in considering the conversion of military positions to civilian positions. This work outlines applies a technique that offers an alternative analytical foundation to that underlying the personnel cost factors promulgated in a regulation issued by the Department of Defense (DoD) Comptroller's office. This document reports new estimates of the economic cost of a military person-year, explains the analytic bases for the new techniques, and describes their implications for a variety of personnel management issues.

An interim report on the material presented here was briefed to Dr. David S. C. Chu, Under Secretary of Defense for Personnel and Readiness, and his staff in August 2005. The method explained in Chapter Three was also applied to specific Army data, and these results have been published by RAND as "Economic Cost of Military Personnel in the Army: Implications for Military-to-Civilian Conversions and Other Personnel Management Issues," by Carl Dahlman and Frank Camm, DB-500-A. Early and interim results of that study were also briefed to Mr. Daniel B. Denning, Acting Assistant Secretary of the Army for Manpower and Reserve Affairs, and his staff on June 22, 2005.

This document should interest policy analysts and decisionmakers concerned with the true cost of military personnel, as well as those concerned with military manpower analysis. The cost estimates generated using the technique described here should have implications for not only military-to-civilian conversion decisions but also a broader set of personnel management issues that arise when we observe personnel costs in this new way.

This research was sponsored by the Office of the Under Secretary of Defense for Personnel and Readiness (OUSD/P&R) and conducted within the Forces and Resources Policy Center of the RAND National Defense Research Institute, a federally funded research and development center sponsored by the Office of the Secretary of Defense, the Joint Staff, the Unified Combatant Commands, the Department of the Navy, the Marine Corps, the defense agencies, and the defense Intelligence Community.

For more information on RAND's Forces and Resources Policy Center, contact the Director, James Hosek. He can be reached by email at James_Hosek@rand.org; by phone at 310-393-0411, extension 7183; or by mail at the RAND Corporation, 1776 Main Street, Santa Monica, California 90407-2138. More information about RAND is available at www.rand.org.

Contents

Figures

Tables

Summary

While it has long been established policy in DoD that military personnel should only be used for military-essential purposes, it has proven difficult to define a concrete boundary that delineates functions that can be performed by civilians in support of military organizations or activities from those that must be performed by military personnel. Often, a discussion of the potential conversion of a particular position or function will turn on the relative cost of a civilian versus a military billet. The presumption has long been that employing a civilian to fill a give position costs less than billeting a military person with similar capability.

This work documents our findings regarding estimating the economic cost of a military person-year and should help to inform the discussion of the relative cost of military and civilian personnel. It presents a new method for estimating the cost of a military person-year and reports the specific findings that emerge when this method if applied to officers and enlisted personnel by year of service (YOS).

Defining the cost of a military person-year for use in comparing with the cost of a civilian may seem like an easy task. However, in practice, a series of choices and computations have to be made that affect the final measures substantially. The cost of a civilian person-year is much simpler to define than that of a military one. The reasons for this can be traced to four basic differences between the two: (1) military compensation is quite complex, combining basic pay with cash and noncash allowances that are often hard to measure properly; (2) compared to civilian pay, military compensation is heavily weighted toward postretirement benefits; (3) military careers are managed through a series of interrelated, sequential assignments, which are generally much shorter than civilian assignments; and (4) military personnel are subject to different work rules (e.g., 24/7 duty hours for the military).

Our research pursued one analytical issue: the cost allocation for accrual for benefits received after retirement. Under the current DoD system, the defense budget does not pay for retirement compensation or for the legislated medical benefits that accrue to Medicare eligibles under the TRICARE For Life (TFL) program. Benefits for qualified retirees are paid out of two trust funds held in the Department of the Treasury and are not considered costs of current military personnel. Instead, DoD pays an annual accrual charge into the trust funds. These accrual charges are carefully calculated actuarial payments that represent the best estimates of the present value of the future costs of current military personnel. Annual accrual charges are deposited in the trust funds, where they will grow, in an accounting sense, to pay the benefits claimed in future years by current military personnel after their retirement.

Under the current system of funding retirement benefits, DoD assesses a flat percentage to the basic monthly paycheck of all military personnel of 31.4 percent, which for fiscal year (FY) 2004 amounted to about $10,500 on the mean basic pay of $33,500. TFL accrual is accomplished on a per capita basis, as the benefits depend only on health status, not on pay. For FY 2004, the DoD accrual assessment for TFL was $5,400 for each member of the military, and it grows at over 6 percent per year, according to officially projected medical inflation rates.

The problem with using the results of this approach when estimating the cost of a person-year is that this method does not take into account either systematic differences in retirement probabilities across the force or the rules for vesting in postretirement benefits. In fact, only a very small proportion (about 15 percent) of an entering cohort of enlisted personnel will ever reach retirement; for officers, the corresponding number is 48 percent. Yet, the current methods of estimating the cost of a person-year essentially treat a first-year enlisted person as having the same probability of reaching retirement eligibility after 20 years of service as someone who has just completed YOS 19. The latter will reach retirement with a likelihood of almost 100 percent, compared to 15 percent for the former, yet the costs are assessed similarly. Likewise, the current DoD cost-allocation system assigns the same costs to a person who has already served 20 years, and therefore does not recognize or account for the fact that such a person is already vested with full benefits.

The method developed over the course of this study, on the other hand, allocates the costs of postretirement benefits in proportion to the likelihood of military personnel reaching vesting. Compared to past methods, our method yields three very significant differences. First, the annual cost of young cohorts (those not yet in the career force) is much lower than official estimates. Second, the cost of personnel with between 10 and 20 YOS (i.e., the cohorts that have a very high likelihood of reaching retirement) increases significantly over official estimates, as our method requires allocating the greatest share of accruing for postretirement benefits to these year-groups. Third, the costs of personnel who have already vested (at YOS 20) become much lower than in official estimates, because the only extra cost our system assigns to them results from relatively small increases in pay due to age and seniority beyond the vesting point. Under the standard method, these people are treated as not having vested at all in the system: clearly a serious error in cost assignment.

The implications for civilianization and force management decisions may be dramatic. First, past civilianization efforts have focused primarily on junior billets. However, if cost is a major factor in civilianization policies, our analysis suggests that the services should focus on civilianizing positions in the career force. In particular, this would entail focusing on positions in grades O-3 to O-5 for officers, and grades E-5 through E-7 for enlisted personnel (see the appendix for titles by grade and service). Second, since the cost of retaining senior personnel is, in reality, much less than officially imputed, the military services should consider whether it is possible to retain more personnel beyond YOS 20. Their annual pay and allowances may be higher, but they cost very little in terms of postretirement benefits; they have already earned most every benefit they would ever be entitled to.

Converting a position from military to civilian has implications for the personnel system. Military careers typically follow fairly precise paths, with the range of choices for each consecutive assignment becoming increasingly narrow as a person moves through the system. Thus, eliminating a military position may cause an emerging hurdle for career management. If a position on the institutional side typically held by an officer or noncommissioned officer (NCO) between two assignments to operational units is eliminated, then not only are there no savings but another billet must be found in which to put that officer or NCO. If the billet were to be a terminal billet, it may be possible to arrange a buyout for someone with less than 20 YOS by using the prior accrued contributions to the retirement system. However, this would do little to ameliorate the career management problem, because that billet should have been available for another personnel assignment at the next rotation cycle. Obviously, real savings occur only if the personnel system can adapt without creating substitute positions after a billet has been eliminated, and that may require long-term changes to current career management practices.

Considerations such as these may lead one to the hypothesis that past civilianizations probably have tended to focus excessively on either junior grades or positions typically filled by personnel already vested in the retirement system. Obviously, conversions of positions with few or no career personnel require less adjustment on the part of the personnel system having to adjust; they also cause less resentment among personnel who were planning on staying 20 years. Unfortunately, information on past conversions by grade is not available, so this hypothesis cannot be tested on actual data.

However, the cost analysis methodology we present here requires the military services not only to decide where to focus their civilianization efforts but also to apply the same principles to developing clear and implementable practices for force management. In the end, the cost of a military billet should play a very small role in any decision to civilianize a military position; these decisions should take place within the larger context of a broad human resources strategy. The issues are what the proper experience mix of the force is and what the cost of seniority ought to be. Under the current system, DoD loses over 40 percent of its senior NCOs and around 25 percent of its officers at YOS 20. Since these high exit rates are driven entirely by the compensation system's vesting requirements (providing 100 percent vesting after 20 YOS and no vesting before that time), it is clear that the experience mix is in no way determined by deliberate force shaping. Rather, the military services have learned to adapt to this rather unique retirement benefits system, which in addition to its vesting provisions has become ever more generous since its inception prior to World War II in the Navy and its adoption by the other services after the war.

The analysis presented here has major implications for force shaping and career management that go far beyond the context of civilianization efforts, whether focused on positions, organizations, or functions. Finally, we should note that the costs included in this work are somewhat incomplete. We have not included health care costs for retirees less than 65 years of age, due to lack of data. Also, although veterans' benefits should, in principle, be included in a complete accrual system, there is no legal provision for doing so; therefore, no methodology has been developed for making the relevant cost estimates.

Acknowledgments

The Under Secretary of Defense for Personnel and Readiness, Dr. David S. C. Chu, conceived and sponsored the research that yielded the analytical techniques that underlie this study. Pam Bartlett, Acting Director of Requirements in OUSD(P&R)/Program Integration, helped shape the underlying research. In the same office, Col. Mark Desens, USMC, was very helpful throughout the project. Assistant Deputy Assistant Secretary of the Army Dr. John Anderson identified the need for the analysis of Army data and contributed critical insights on segments of the project focused on Army data. I thank them all for their support and insights.

Mr. Joel Sitrin, DoD chief actuary, generously helped to explain the data and methods that the actuaries use. Mr. Kevin Lannon, manpower specialist in OUSD(Comptroller), helped us understand the construction of the comptroller rates used here. He also corrected several errors. At RAND, Jennifer Pace put together the Army data used for this analysis. John Christian carried out much of the data analysis supporting the results. RAND colleagues Beth Asch, Ray Conley, Lionel Galway, Mike Hix, Jacob Klerman, Chip Leonard, Bruce Orvis, Ellen Pint, and Al Robbert have patiently worked through various iterations of the analysis. Denny Eakle, Director of the 10th Quadrennial Review of Military Compensation, gave insightful comments on the final draft.

My greatest debt is to my colleague Frank Camm, coauthor on the Army part of the project. His dedication to applying the best economic analysis to defense management of commercial activities and outsourcing has long standing and is widely respected. His ideas and influence on this project permeate much of the analysis and presentation in this study.

My colleagues Greg Hildebrandt, Edward Keating, and Jim Hosek provided many valuable comments in their reviews, which led to a series of significant clarifications of certain obscure points in the analysis as well as to the corrections of various errors, misguided opinions, and overzealous formulations. I thank them for their assistance and collegiality.

While I am grateful to everyone for their contributions, I retain full responsibility for the accuracy and objectivity of the findings and conclusions reported here.

Abbreviations

AEAN	Aggregate Entry Age Normal
CBO	Congressional Budget Office
CJR	career job reservation
CPI	Consumer Price Index
DoD	Department of Defense
DOS	date of separation
DVA	Department of Veterans Affairs
E-COMP	economic compensation
ENL	enlisted personnel
FASAB	Federal Accounting Standards Advisory Board
FASB	Financial Accounting Standards Board
FERS	Federal Employee Retirement System
FG	federal government
FSB	force shaping board
FY	fiscal year
FYDP	Future Years Defense Program
GAO	Government Accountability Office

LADSC	limited active-duty service commitment
NSPS	National Security Personnel System
OACT	Office of the Actuary (DoD)
OFF	officer
OMB	Office of Management and Budget
OSD	Office of the Secretary of Defense
OUSD/P&R	Office of the Under Secretary of Defense for Personnel and Readiness
PA&E	Office of Program Analysis and Evaluation (OSD)
PV	present discounted value
RIF	reduction in force
RMC	regular military compensation
SERB	selective early retirement board
SMCR	Standard Military Composite Rate
TDA	Table of Distribution and Allowances
TO&E	Table of Organization and Equipment
TFL	TRICARE for Life
TPV	total present value
VSP	voluntary separation program
YOS	years of service

CHAPTER ONE

Introduction

A basic principle in the Department of Defense (DoD) has always been to only use military personnel for military-essential tasks. However, the boundary between military-essential and civilian tasks can never be perfectly clear; several considerations invariably leave the definition of military-essential open to interpretation. Still, the policy guidance from the Office of the Secretary of Defense (OSD) recommending the civilianization of ever-more functions and positions has been consistent.[1] This guidance stems from both the aforementioned principle and from budgetary considerations—OSD has long believed that military personnel cost more than comparable civilians. Although the cost of manpower is only one of the drivers of civilianization policies, it is never absent from the discussion to determine which functions and positions should be converted from military to civilian. However, cost has proven to be a somewhat murky subject in the continued development and execution of civilianization policies.

Civilianizing military positions has never been simple in execution, even when pursued diligently. As a policy, civilianization can only be properly applied when it is an integral element of a broader personnel-management strategy. In some contexts, civilianization may be driven

1 See U.S. Department of Defense, "Guidance for Manpower Management," Department of Defense Directive 1100.4, February 12, 2005; and U.S. Department of Defense, "Guidance for Determining Workforce Mix," Department of Defense Directive 1100.22, September 7, 2006. The fundamental principle behind this guidance is that costs must be weighed against risk and operational effectiveness. Obviously, this leaves wide latitude in implementation.

by a desire to reduce expenditures on military personnel, in which case it would seem appropriate to first civilianize the most costly functions and then to follow up by eliminating the authorizations for the affected military positions. In other contexts, a service may find it necessary to transfer military authorizations from infrastructure or support activities to positions more closely engaged in warfighting, which may only be possible if the affected support functions are civilianized. In the first case, the desire to reduce total personnel costs may be the driving factor; in the second, cost analysis may be essential only to identify the budgetary implications of the policy. In either case, the new measures of person-year costs that we have developed provide a better foundation for the development of a broad, force-shaping strategy than previously available measures. Our measures may not only assist in targeting the right positions for civilianization but also help to identify the personnel actions required to support the strategy.

The task before us was to develop a more solid foundation for costing out a military service year; in doing so, we hope to resolve the continuing controversy over whether military personnel or civilian are more expensive, and by how much. We had to scale conceptual as well as computational hurdles to achieve our goal. For example, the word *cost* requires a more precise definition than it has hitherto been afforded in standard budgetary terminology. Also, the actual cost of military manpower differs depending on whether we are considering the cost to DoD alone or the cost to the entire federal government (FG).

Throughout this work, we use the term *economic cost* to connote that our calculations are more reflective of the concept of opportunity cost in the field of economics. That is, we contend that our cost estimates are closer to the actual cost of a person-year than previous estimates and that they are therefore better estimates of the actual savings the federal government would achieve by civilianizing a military position. Conversely, our estimates also provide a better reflection of the cost of retaining a person—the proper meaning of *opportunity cost* in the context of sourcing decisions (i.e., whether a position should be military or civilian).[2]

Our approach to allocating present budget costs using basic economic principles differs from standard DoD practice.[3] As outlined in Chapter Two, there is some concern that total cost estimates developed using DoD Comptroller regulations are not quite correct. However, the major problem with the current DoD rules for determining the cost of a military person-year is that total cost is incorrectly allocated across working years. Thus, even if the total cost of military personnel were correctly estimated (as they currently are not[4]), DoD's cost allocation rules would still give an incorrect estimate of the real cost of a person-year. Our revised method shows that the person-year costs for some positions are systematically over- or underestimated by official cost estimates. Since cost is nearly always a consideration in civilianization (either in targeting functions or positions or in evaluating the budgetary impact of civilianization decisions made for reasons other than cost), reliance on official estimates may result in civilianization efforts focused on areas of lesser payoff or in the miscalculation of the real budgetary implications of civilianization decisions. Thus, our results are of significant relevance even in civilianization efforts where cost is

---

2 There are other possible notions of *opportunity cost*, depending on the context of a particular decision. For an individual considering staying for another year in the military, the opportunity cost of leaving is the value of his or her compensation package that year plus (or minus) the subjective value he or she places on military service; for a service, the opportunity cost of retaining a member for another year is his or her compensation plus the cost of any education and training resources that would yield returns only over future years; for DoD, the opportunity cost is only that part of personnel costs that are included in the DoD budget—it excludes costs budgeted by other agencies.

3 Our approach builds on the method developed by Adele R. Palmer and David J. Osbaldeston (see Adele R. Palmer and David J. Osbaldeston, *Incremental Costs of Military and Civilian Manpower in the Military Services*, Santa Monica, Calif.: RAND Corporation, N-2677-FMP, 1988). It also benefited from the analyses presented in William M. Hix and William W. Taylor, *A Policymaker's Guide to Accrual Funding of Military Retirement*, Santa Monica, Calif.: RAND Corporation, MR-760-A, 1997; and Susan A. Gates and Albert A. Robbert, *Comparing the Costs of DoD Military and Civil Service Personnel*, Santa Monica, Calif.: RAND Corporation, MR-980-OSD, 1998.

4 We demonstrate this point below. Briefly, much of the actual costs of military personnel either are not identified as such in the DoD budget or are outside the DoD budget entirely.

not the primary driving factor: Credit awarded in the budget process to civilianization efforts using current DoD cost estimating practices will be systematically skewed upward or downward from actual long-term cost savings, depending on what positions are converted.

However, the major implication of our alternative calculus is that truly effective *force management*—using strategic human-resources principles to identify the proper mix of age and experience in the personnel inventory—requires an increased focus on the cost of personnel. The civilianization of military positions is only one of the many tools that can and should be used to shape the force, and the cost calculus presented here is but one element of effective civilianization activities. However, the proper calculus of personnel cost estimates should be a major focus in the larger issue of how to construct and implement a general human-resources management strategy for the military. Force shaping and personnel management, especially retention decisions, need to include a more complete calculus of the true economic cost of military personnel. Our analysis provides an important step in the right direction, if implemented appropriately in policy guidance from OSD and executed in the budget submissions prepared by the military services.

CHAPTER TWO

Personnel Costs and DoD-Regulated Conversion Rates

In this chapter, we discuss the component elements of military compensation and relate them to budgetary outlays by DoD and other federal agencies. We also analyze the fairly crude estimates of the cost of a military person-year that result from the application of these data. We then present the official DoD costs of military person-years for use in conversions of military positions to civilian (i.e., the cost estimates developed using the DoD-mandated calculus) and discuss some of their shortcomings.

Estimating the Cost of Military Personnel Using the DoD-Mandated Calculus

No system used to compensate federal government employees is simple, but the system used to compensate military personnel is by far the most complex. There are approximately 90 different pay systems for various kinds of specialized civilian personnel, some specific to individual agencies.[1] There is only one pay system for military personnel. While this system is common to all the military services, it comprises

[1] This does not count the most recent (and perhaps most audacious) pay system: the National Security Personnel System (NSPS). The NSPS is being implemented for a large segment of the DoD workforce. For more information on this initiative, see U.S. Department of Defense, Civilian Personnel Management System, "National Personnel Management System," Web site, February 1, 2007.

many different kinds of pay and entitlements. In a recent report, the U.S. Government Accountability Office (GAO) expressed it this way:

> The military compensation system has had the same basic structure since the end of World War II, but over time, it has become a complex and piecemeal culmination and accretion of pay, benefits, and special tax preferences—each designed to meet a specific need in managing an evolving force. Today, the total military compensation package includes dozens of pays and allowances; several non-cash benefits to take care of troops who, increasingly, are married with children; certain preferences; as well as lifetime retirement pay and health care for retirees and their families. Valuing military service is complicated.[2]

Added to the complexities of an arcane and patchwork compensation system is the fact that not all personnel costs are paid out as direct monetary remuneration. When comparing the cost of a military position against that of a civilian position, whether filled by a federal government civilian employee or a hired contractor, all these costs should, in principle, be computed and compared. Table 2.1 shows most of the fiscal year (FY) 2005 federal budgetary costs (in thousands of dollars) for military personnel, along with a heuristic computation of the cost of a military person-year.

Table 2.1 illustrates not only the multiple elements of cash and noncash compensation received by current military personnel in FY 2005 but also the complex patchwork of deferred compensation and various benefits and services available to military personnel after their retirement. Depending on which of these cost elements are included, the FY 2005 valuation of an average military person-year ranges from about $58,000 to over $175,000. Achieving greater precision clearly requires making analytical choices relevant to the particular situation at hand. When considering whether or not to civilianize a function or position, the basic determinant should be the military personnel costs

---

[2] U.S. Government Accountability Office, *Military Personnel: DoD Needs to Improve the Transparency and Reassess the Reasonableness, Appropriateness, Affordability, and Sustainability of Its Military Compensation System*, Washington, D.C., GAO-05-798, July 2005, p. 1.

Table 2.1
Elements of Military Compensation and Personnel Costs, Fiscal Year 2005

	FY 2005 Cost	Cost Per Work-Year
Current compensation costs		
Cash		
Basic pay	$42,001,244	
Basic allowance for housing (BAH)	$11,539,905	
Basic allowance for subsistence	$2,994,794	
Special and incentive pays	$3,417,392	
Allowances	$2,064,392	
Other pays and allowances	$26,984	
Social Security tax	$3,191,640	
Income tax tenefits (Dept. of Treasury)	$2,407,441	
Subtotal	$67,643,792	$47,840
In-kind benefits		
Health care, current dependents	$5,121,293	
Family housing	$4,345,365	
Personal travel	$1,701,701	
Subsistence in-kind (SIK)	$1,312,494	
Child education (Dept. of Education)	$437,219	
Education assistance, current	$636,284	
Discount groceries, current	$366,279	
Child development	$684,272	
Family support services	$186,900	
Transportation subsidy	$18,844	
Subtotal	$14,810,651	
Total current compensation costs	$82,454,443	$58,315

Table 2.1—Continued

	FY 2005 Cost	Cost Per Work-Year
Deferred compensation costs		
Cash		
Retired pay accrual	$11,545,160	
Separation pay	$828,378	
Special compensation for disabled	$0	
Unemployment benefits	$241,798	
Death gratuities	$13,985	
Survivor benefits	$10,295	
Veterans' benefits, cash (Dept. of VA)	$32,422,146	
Concurrent receipt (Dept. of Treasury)	$1,477,226	
Subtotal	$46,538,988	
In-kind benefits		
Health care, deferred	$9,062,646	
Defense Health Plan (DHP) accrual	$7,442,940	
Discount groceries, deferred	$470,802	
Separation travel	$456,910	
Education assistance, deferred	$17,276	
Veterans' benefits, in-kind (Dept of VA)	$31,634,652	
Employment training (Dept of Labor)	$222,833	
Subtotal	$49,308,059	
Total deferred compensation costs	$95,847,047	
Total compensation costs	$178,301,490	$126,101
Non-compensation costs		
Health care, current military personnel	$4,214,822	
Training (including cadets and ROTC)	$4,446,398	

Table 2.1—Continued

	FY 2005 Cost	Cost Per Work-Year
Base operations support (BOS), facilities, and support for training	$2,272,620	
Child education	$1,515,367	
Operational travel	$893,103	
Recruitment, advertising, etc.	$1,135,527	
Manpower management	$728,111	
Other personnel support	$548,427	
Other costs	$6,111	
Total non-compensation costs	$15,760,486	$67,787
Total current personnel costs	$194,061,976	$137,248
Legacy costs		
Retired pay (Dept. of Treasury)	$36,984,891	
Health care (Dept. of Treasury)	$16,312,000	
Total legacy costs	$53,296,891	
Total outlays for Miltiary Personnel	$247,358,867	$174,941
Average work-years	1,413,953	

SOURCE: OSD Office of Program Analysis and Evaluation (PA&E).

NOTE: Data are budget estimates, not execution data.

avoided by this action. If a similar calculus can then be performed for an alternative civilian position, the costs of each course of action can be compared and net savings from proposed conversions estimated.

Cash and Legacy Costs

Beginning from the top left of Table 2.1, it is obvious that all *current compensation* (i.e., compensation paid in the year in which it is earned), whether cash or noncash, represents a cost of current military personnel, so the baseline cost of a military person-year is around $58,000. It is equally obvious that the legacy costs for retirement and health shown at the bottom right of the table would be unaffected by any civilianization decision affecting current military personnel, since they represent payments to personnel already retired from military service. Therefore, these costs should not be included in the computation of the cost of a current military person-year. Eliminating legacy costs from the calculus, the savings that could be obtained from civilianizing an average military position are therefore around $137,000 per year, at a maximum.

Deferred Costs

The elements listed as deferred compensation are various personnel costs funded in a number of different ways. A total of roughly $19 billion are appropriated in the DoD military personnel budget as accrual costs for retirement and health benefits that will be paid out only to those who qualify for retirement after 20 years of service (YOS).[3] These accrual amounts represent the current cost of paying future benefits. If a military position is civilianized, the accrual cost of that position is avoided, so it appears that we must include accrual costs when calculating the cost of a current military person-year.[4]

Table 2.1 also shows other elements of deferred compensation for which there currently is no accrual system. The biggest such expense indicated in the table is the outlay by the Department of Veterans Affairs (DVA), totaling around $64 billion in FY 2005 and consisting of both

---

[3] The data in Table 2.1 were identified by analysts from OSD's Office of Program Analysis and Evaluation (PA&E), and we have not changed them in our displays. However, one significant element of the legacy costs is absent. In addition to accrual, the U.S. Department of the Treasury is obligated by law to request appropriations for the payment of interest on all federal trust fund assets, including the Military Retirement and TRICARE For Life (TFL) Trust Funds (the biggest federal trust funds are those associated with Social Security and Medicare). For completeness, these interest payments should also be included in this calculus as costs of accrual, and this would add another $17 billion to the total. However, since this entire methodology for estimating person-year costs may be flawed (as demonstrated in Chapter Three), we set aside this particular concern.

[4] Since appearances are often deceiving, we feel obligated to point out that we argue in Chapters Five and Six that trust fund assets are only intragovernmental transfers and not costs at all, even though their accrual appears as budget outlays on agency books. Costs and budget outlays should not be confused with one another.

cash benefits and various medical and rehabilitation services offered to qualifying veterans. Since there is currently no accrual system for veterans' benefits and these expenses constitute payments to personnel who have left military service (i.e., they are really legacy costs, on par with retirement pay and TFL medical benefits), they should not be included in the cost of present military personnel. If it were possible to compute a reasonable accrual equivalent for the DVA expenditures (as DoD indeed does for retirement pay and TFL benefits), then that would be a better cost element to include than the total DVA outlay now shown. However, such a computation would be very complex, requiring projections of the probability of current military personnel becoming eligible for future veterans' benefits and the projected costs of those benefits, including health services, over their remaining lifetimes. For illustrative purposes, a very simple comparison can be made by dividing the FY 2005 accrual for military retired compensation ($11.5 billion) by the total legacy outlays for currently retired military personnel ($37.5 billion), which yields a ratio of a little over 30 percent. If this same ratio were to hold for veterans' benefits (and there is no particular reason to assume that it should), then no more than about $20 billion should be assessed as the accrual-equivalent cost of funding future veterans' benefits for current military personnel. Although the correct annual accrual amount cannot be computed at the present time, by virtue of the compound interest accretion inherent in accrual accounting, it is very likely to be less than the $64 billion paid out by DVA in 2005, even though current contingencies in Iraq and Afghanistan have increased the number of potential beneficiaries.[5]

The same argument holds true for the remaining almost $13 billion of outlays for deferred compensation, whether cash or noncash. In Table 2.1, they are represented as the current cost of providing various benefits and services, as they are included in the DoD budget; however, these outlays are really legacy costs paid out to personnel who

---

[5] Any actuarial estimate of currently required accrual payments made to create a fund for the payment of future disability payments would obviously be very sensitive to the prevalence and nature of future conflicts: A computation based on data for the last 50 years would be only a starting point. The nature of modern warfare and modern casualty treatment options have changed the ratio and cost of deaths and disabilities drastically.

have left military service. The correct method for estimating the current costs of these benefits would be to compute an accrual-equivalent, again requiring extensive analysis of the probabilities of various personnel claiming the benefits after they have left service and the future costs of those benefits. For now, it suffices to conclude that it would be analytically incorrect to incorporate these costs into any estimate of the cost of a current military person-year, as only some currently unknown fraction should be assessed as an imputed accrual amount.

Noncompensation Costs

In principle, the almost $17 billion in noncompensation costs shown in Table 2.1 represent current costs for all military personnel, and it might appear that a portion of these training, current health-care, base-support, and management costs could be avoided for each civilianized military position. However, it is not clear that eliminating a few thousand positions throughout one or another of the military services would affect the cost estimate of a military person-year to a noticeable degree, since such overhead costs are generally not affected by small changes in the total number of military positions. Unless a civilianization decision affects a large swath of activities, so large that institutional and management activities also change significantly, there is no reason to expect the noncompensation costs in Table 2.1 would change at all. These are the most difficult cost elements to evaluate when assessing the savings to be gained from civilianizing military positions. Indeed, for small civilianization efforts, it is best if they are left out of the computations entirely.

In conclusion, using the figures provided in Table 2.1, the cost of a military person-year includes compensation costs plus known accrual costs, which for FY 2005 were $58,315 plus $13,429, equaling $71,744 per military person. However, this amount does not include the cost of the accrual of certain future benefits and costs. Using a range of accrual rates for these cost elements of between 20 and 40 percent, a very crude estimate of their costs would add between $11,000 and $22,000 per person. The midpoint estimate of the total cost of an average military position is therefore around $87,000 per year (plus or minus approximately $6,000, for a range of $81,000 to $93,000). Although this is a very crude estimate, it is likely somewhat nearer the truth than a figure derived by attributing legacy costs and fixed overhead costs to the cost of current military personnel. However, as we shall show in some detail below, this crude number is still off by a considerable margin, even though it would seem to be roughly consistent with the data in Table 2.1. Unfortunately, there are additional costs lurking beneath the surface for which we have not yet not accounted.

DoD-Mandated Cost Factors

An exercise such as the one outlined above using the data shown in Table 2.1 has very limited practical value in efforts to determine a cost factor for a military person-year; it was included here mainly to illustrate the complexity involved in producing such an estimate. An analysis of Table 2.1 does demonstrate that the military pay system is very complex. It also shows that personnel costs and compensation elements are not easily identified in budget displays but have to be cobbled together from various parts of the federal budget. Furthermore, even if an analytically solid estimate of the average cost of a military person-year could be produced via such an analysis, it would be of little use in practice, as every particular instance of a proposed conversion of a function or position from military to civilian is likely to deviate substantially from the average.

For these reasons, the DoD Comptroller developed Standard Military Composite Rates (SMCRs), a set of grade-specific cost factors for military personnel. Under DoD regulations, these are the rates to be used for use in cost calculations undertaken for civilianization purposes.[6] In the SMCRs, the cost of a military person-year is equal to a metric called regular military compensation (RMC). RMC includes average basic pay for each military grade, basic allowance for housing, basic allowance for subsistence, and federal tax advantage accruing to the aforementioned allowances because they are not subject to federal

[6] U.S. Department of Defense, Office of the Under Secretary of Defense (Comptroller), "Military Composite Standard Pay and Reimbursement Rates, Fiscal Year 2005," September 16, 2004.

income tax.[7] The prescribed rates are shown in Figure 2.1 and Table 2.2.

Compared with the average cost of a military person-year derived from Table 2.1 in the previous section, these rates have the obvious advantage of giving different values for different grades. Since the variation in pay and allowances is quite wide—varying by a factor of around 3.5 from lowest to highest for enlisted personnel and officers separately and by a factor of 6 for all grades considered together—it is clearly important to use rates by grade when calculating the applicable personnel costs in each particular civilianization scenario. In this sense, the SMCRs are clearly a step in the right direction.

Figure 2.1
DoD Comptroller's Standard Military Composite Rates

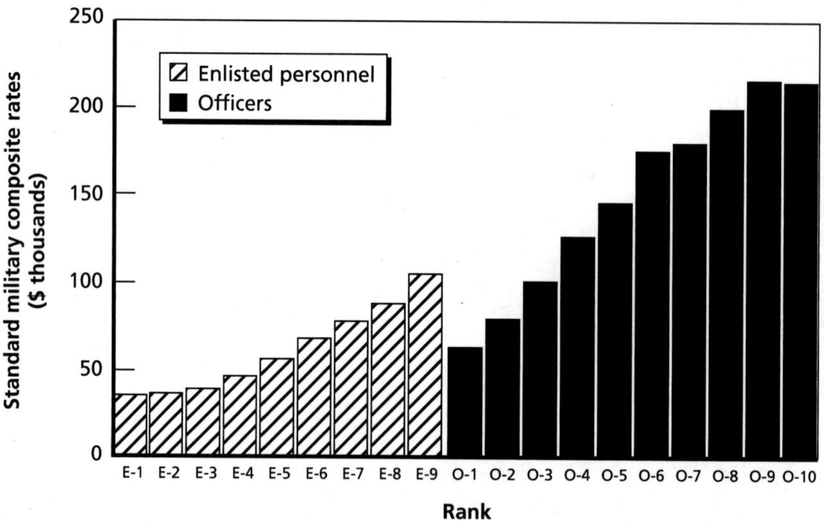

SOURCE: U.S. Department of Defense, Office of the Under Secretary of Defense (Comptroller), "Military Composite Standard Pay and Reimbursement Rates, Fiscal Year 2005," September 16, 2004.
RAND *MG598-2.1*

7 See United States Code, Title 37, Section 101(25), January 3, 2005.

Table 2.2
DoD Comptroller's Standard Military Composite Rates

Grade	Annual Pay Rate
Enlisted Personnel	
E-1	$34,785
E-2	$36,498
E-3	$38,879
E-4	$46,044
E-5	$55,713
E-6	$67,628
E-7	$78,116
E-8	$88,733
E-9	$104,933
Officers	
O-1	$62,982
O-2	$78,991
O-3	$100,883
O-4	$126,746
O-5	$145,941
O-6	$175,928
O-7	$180,720
O-8	$199,215
O-9	$215,758
O-10	$215,043

SOURCE: U.S. Department of Defense, Office of the Under Secretary of Defense (Comptroller), "Military Composite Standard Pay and Reimbursement Rates, Fiscal Year 2005," September 16, 2004.

NOTE: OSD (Comptroller) informs these values are based on samples from Army data only. It is therefore possible that they are different than samples based on all services would yield. Since we are only using the data for illustrative purposes, any (likely small) bias resulting from limited sampling is of little consequence.

Combining the SMCRs with data on the existing inventory of enlisted personnel and officers by grade gives

- an enlisted personnel weighted average SMCR of $52,915
- an officer weighted average SMCR of $109,034
- a weighted average SMCR across all military personnel of $61,393.

If the crude estimate of the cost of a military person-year (including all reasonable costs over and beyond the SMC) generated by the analysis of the data in Table 2.1 discussed in the previous section is accurate, the Comptroller's prescribed SMCRs are off by between one-third and one-half ($61,000 versus a range $81,000 to $93,000). This does not necessarily mean that it is entirely inappropriate to use the DoD Comptroller's SMCRs in the analysis of civilianization decisions, since the Comptroller's cost estimates are specifically intended to include only those personnel costs that are appropriated in the DoD budget and intentionally leave out costs that are funded in the budgets of other federal entities. However, using the data in Table 2.1, it is possible to perform a simple check on the SMCRs by adding up cash and allowances (RMC), the accrual amounts for health and retirement, and unemployment reimbursements to the U.S. Department of Labor and dividing the sum by the total military population. This yields a DoD budget relevant per capita cost of $71,915, as compared with an average prescribed SMCR of only $61,393, which is clearly problematic: Using the Comptroller's own methods as mandated by DoD financial management regulations, it appears that the published SMCRs are actually off by 20 percent. This is not guesswork; this figure was generated using official DoD data and methods. However, this will actually turn out to be a very minor point; as we shall demonstrate below, there are deeper and more fundamental problems with the SMCRs. We have therefore not attempted to trace the source of the errors in the official numbers.

Finally, we note a significant problem with the SMCRs. As mentioned, they include accrual as a budget cost to DoD, which in turn implies that accrual is a cost to the FG, clearly ignoring the fact that accrual payments, although they are indeed made by DoD, are counted as revenue by the Department of the Treasury. From the standpoint of the FG, accrual is therefore not a cost at all but rather an intragovernmental transfer payment—the movement of money from one budget account to another. Hence, including accrual payments in estimates of the cost to the FG of a military person-year is simply wrong and provides very misleading figures. Thus, while their actuarial allocation of accrual payments by retirement probabilities is a step in the right direction, SMCRs are still not correct estimates of the real cost of a military person-year.

CHAPTER THREE

The Cost of Deferred Compensation

This chapter describes the accrual methods used by actuaries in the DoD Office of Actuary (OACT) and discusses the problems that arise when these methods are used to estimate the cost of a military person-year. It then presents a more economically accurate alternative approach that allocates total accrual charges across person-years.

The Principle and Practice of Accrual Funding

The military retirement system is a defined benefit plan that provides for vesting after 20 YOS on active duty.[1] The plan has several elements, of which the major ones are retirement income and postretirement health benefits. Although there are other benefits—veterans' benefits, commissary rights, etc.—they are not considered here for reasons the discussed in Chapter Two.

Undoubtedly, the most important retirement benefit for military personnel is retirement income. Unlike most private and public retirement plans (and unlike the retirement plan for reserve military personnel), retirement income annuities to qualified active-duty retirees begin immediately upon retirement and are not tied to age. From the time of the Navy's first retirement payments in 1938 (and in the Army and Air Force after World War II) through the early 1980s, all benefits to military retirees were paid out of yearly DoD budget appropriations;

[1] Since the focus of this work is on the methods for costing military person-years in the context of civilianization studies, it does not address retirement accrual issues for reservists.

in other words, benefits were funded through a pay-as-you-go system. Public Law 98-94, enacted in 1983, established a military retirement trust fund in FY 1985 from which benefits to retirees would henceforth be paid.[2] DoD became responsible for budgeting for the accrual of money to this fund on behalf of current military personnel, and a DoD Retirement Board of Actuaries was established to certify that correct appropriations were included in the budgets that the President submitted to Congress. Since then, the figure that DoD has included in its annual budget submission to Congress to augment the Military Retirement Trust Fund (which is kept on the books of the Department of Treasury) has amounted to only a percentage of current total military pay. All payments to retirees are made from this fund.

The second most important military retirement benefit is free health care for qualifying retirees. Congress expanded the health benefits available to Medicare-eligible military retirees and their dependents with the creation of TFL in the FY 2001 National Defense Authorization Act.[3] The TFL program became available to eligible beneficiaries on October 1, 2001. The same law also created a DoD Health Board of Actuaries and provided for a trust fund mechanism similar to that for retirement income. DoD was made responsible for paying into the trust fund the actuarially correct amount required to fund future benefits for currently employed military personnel; all benefits for presently eligible retirees would then be paid out of the fund account. Since this account is held by the Department of the Treasury, benefits payments to retirees do not encumber the DoD budget; DoD would budget only for accrual payments for current military personnel.

For both the military retirement and TFL trust funds, the relevant statutes mandate that the actuarial computations of funding requirements apply a particular accrual method called Aggregate Entry Age

---

[2] Currently incorporated into law as United States Code, Title 10, Chapter 74, "Military Retirement Trust Fund," January 3, 2005. For a brief history of the military retirement system, see Appendix B in U.S. Department of Defense, Office of the Actuary, *Valuation of the Military Retirement System*, Arlington, Va., September 30, 2004.

[3] Public Law 106-398, H.R. 5408, *Floyd D. Spence National Defense Authorization Act for FY 2001*, Section 713, Chapter 56.

Normal (AEAN).[4] Using figures calculated under AEAN, the trust funds receive annual payments for each service member while that service member is on active duty (there are parallel arrangements for reserve forces); these payments, plus market-based interest payments paid by the FG on the net assets in the fund, are intended to be sufficient to cover the future payment of benefits to all current service members. The AEAN method is applied to each new cohort of entrants, and payments into the fund are stretched out over all the working years of the cohort.

The annual contribution charged to payroll to fund future benefits is called the *normal cost*. The normal cost concept was first implemented by DoD in the Military Retirement Trust Fund as follows:

$$NC_{pension} = \frac{PV(B_{it})}{PV(C_{it})} \tag{3.1}$$

Here, the normal cost ($NC_{pension}$) is the ratio of the present discounted value of all future benefit payments (B, here representing pension payments) to all eligible individuals (subscript i) in the entry cohort for all future time periods (subscript t), divided by the present discounted value of earnings for these individuals' working life (C). Both the numerator and the denominator are measured in dollars. Equation 3.1 illustrates the defining characteristic of the AEAN methodology: The evaluation of a ratio of two present values, with the numerator representing the future benefit payments and the denominator representing the future salaries on the basis of which the benefits are earned.

In Equation 3.1, the numerator is always less than the denominator for two reasons. First, benefits are set at a much lower level than annual earnings; second, the employment compensation in the denominator is paid out during the working life of cohort members, but the benefits are paid out after retirement, so that the numerator is discounted to the present over a more distant future time period than the denominator. The normal cost computed by evaluating this ratio

---

[4] The AEAN method is one of several in a group known as cost approaches. As we will report in Chapter Six, AEAN is not recommended for use in private sector defined benefit plans but has been defended as appropriate for public plans.

using data on benefits and costs is then applied to the entire wage bill for the budget year, making the total normal cost equal to a percentage of present payroll that will be deposited in the trust fund. Obviously, this means that higher contributions are made on behalf of individuals who earn higher salaries, which is entirely appropriate if the benefits to be paid out in later years are also proportional to the salaries that individuals receive while working, as are the benefits paid out from the military retirement trust fund. Since retired pay to military personnel is a share of basic pay earned while in uniform, the normal cost contribution is set at a fixed percentage that is applied to the individual's pay at each point on the pay scale.[5]

In contrast to pension benefits, health benefits are not related to pay or grade but only to YOS.[6] Regardless of their earnings while working, all eligible individuals will be entitled to exactly the same benefits under TFL. Therefore, the DoD Health Board of Actuaries chose to implement an alternative interpretation of the standard normal cost formula shown earlier in Equation 3.1 for TFL:

$$NC_{TFL} = \frac{PV(B_{it})}{PV(N_{it})} \tag{3.2}$$

In Equation 3.2, the numerator is measured in dollars, but the denominator is measured in person-years; thus, the denominator is interpreted as the present discounted value of all future working years of the individuals in the entry cohort.[7] In other words, here the charge

---

5 For further details on the benefit rules and actuarial computations for military retirement benefits, see DoD, Office of the Actuary, *Valuation of the Military Retirement System*.

6 For a detailed discussion of TFL benefits, see Michael Schoenbaum, Barbara O. Wynn, Terri Tanielian, Katherine M. Harris, Renee Labor, and C. Ross Anthony, *Health Benefits for Medicare Eligible Military Retirees: Rationalizing TRICARE for Life*, Santa Monica, Calif.: RAND Corporation, TR-118-OSD, 2004; U.S. Department of Defense, Office of the Assistant Secretary of Defense (Health Affairs), and the TRICARE Management Activity, "TRICARE for Life," Web site, October 12, 2006; and Military.com, "TRICARE for Life," Web page, n.d.

7 Discounting is a method used when making comparisons of values (dollars or utility) across different time periods and is required because the same amount in the future has

is a per capita charge in current dollars that is not affected by pay grade but is instead equal for all employees.[8]

To estimate the present contribution required to fund future benefits at the right level, the actuarial method must make projections regarding a series of critical variables that can be divided into three basic categories: demographic, programmatic, and economic. The most important demographic variables are

- the size of each entry cohort, broken out by officers and enlisted personnel
- YOS patterns, which determine benefits eligibility and pension levels for retired personnel and their dependents
- patterns of mortality for retirees and their dependents until the such time as last member of the cohort or dependent of a member of the cohort is deceased

---

greater value the closer it is to the present. That is, discounting future dollars to the present is a way to account for this time-dependent valuation. It is unusual to see discounting applied to work-years, which do not have a dollar value attached to them. According to the OACT, this particular procedure was chosen in order to stay consistent with the requirement in the statute to use a version of the AEAN method (DoD, Office of the Actuary, *Valuation of the Military Retirement System*). Since the AEAN method is the computation of a ratio between two present values, the denominator must be a discounted value; hence, the DoD formula introduces the unusual notion of discounting work-years, not dollar values. In strict economic terms, this means that the denominator is not a present value at all, since it has no values attached to it; hence, it may not be a true AEAN formula.

[8] In principle, the number of years used in the denominator is a matter of choice; for instance, the payments for the projected benefits of the entry cohort can be taken in a series of payments over the working life of the cohort, or they can be taken in one single year (e.g., the initial working year). In the former case, the contributions to the trust fund are spread over a period of years, with the fraction attributed to each successive cohort in the inventory shrinking as people exit the active-duty workforce for various reasons. In the latter case, an initial contribution is levied against a given cohort's entire payroll in one year and then set aside to earn interest until the members of that cohort who qualify for TFL (e.g., after 20 years of active-duty service) become eligible for benefits (e.g., by reaching age 65 and enrolling in Medicare Part B). Thus, there are various ways to implement Equation 3.2 while remaining broadly consistent with the overall notion of charging a sufficient initial amount that grows with interest so that all later benefits can be paid from the accumulated assets of the trust fund.

- patterns of disability that lead to disability pay or Medicare eligibility
- patterns of marriage, divorce, and remarriage, determining dependents' pension and TFL benefits.

These demographic variables are projected by age and sex for the entry cohort across its active-duty service years, at retirement eligibility at 20 YOS, and up to the statutory maximum of 35 YOS. Also, marriage and divorce rates and fertility rates are projected to determine the likely number of eligible dependents, and mortality and disability rates are estimated and projected. The result is a prospective future demographic history of the entire cohort through the death of its last member at an expected age of 110. Since the youngest entrant may be under 18 and the youngest eligible dependent may not be born until many years after the primary beneficiary has retired, these projections require forecasting demographic variable over time span of more than 100 years. Figures 3.1 and 3.2 illustrate the nature of the basic projection for the primary beneficiaries in entering cohorts of active-duty enlisted personnel and officers in their first service year.

In the actuaries' steady-state projections, the entering cohort of enlisted personnel is almost 166,000 per year; the entering cohort of officers is a little over 11,000 per year.[9] Of these, 15.7 percent of enlisted personnel and 48 percent of officers are projected to stay long enough to become vested in postretirement benefits at YOS 20 (and some of these will continue to serve until the statutory maximum at YOS 35). As personnel retire, the size of the beneficiary pool increases until a age 53 for enlisted personnel and age 58 for officers, after which the annual death rate gradually depletes the inventory until the last member of the cohort passes away at age 110. At age 65, the TFL-eligible population becomes equal to the retired population. In addition to these forecasts of the primary population, there are similar projections of the number of dependents who will be eligible for benefits (survivors' benefits for

[9] Because of the practice of allowing constructive credit for prior service to some newly commissioned officers (e.g., graduates of the military academies) and the possibility of transfers from enlisted ranks to the officer corps, there are more officers in the second, third, and fourth YOS than in the first.

Figure 3.1
Actuarial Projection of the Primary Population, Enlisted

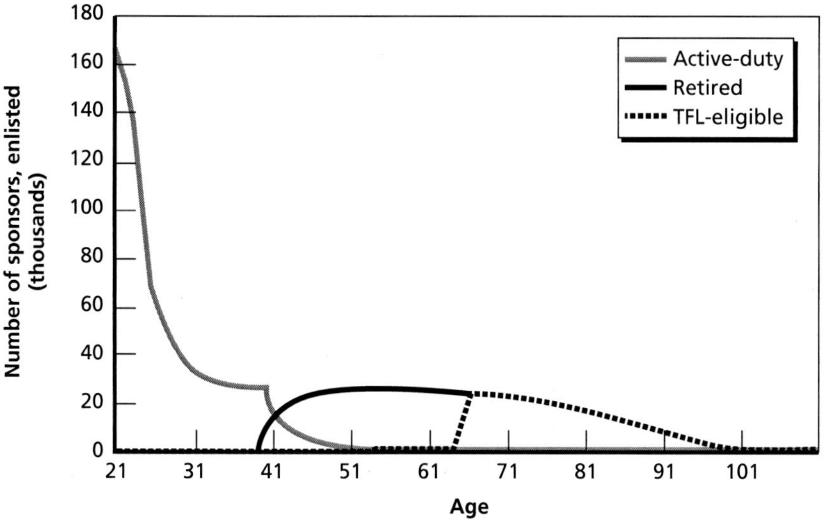

RAND *MG598-3.1*

Figure 3.2
Actuarial Projection of the Primary Population, Officers

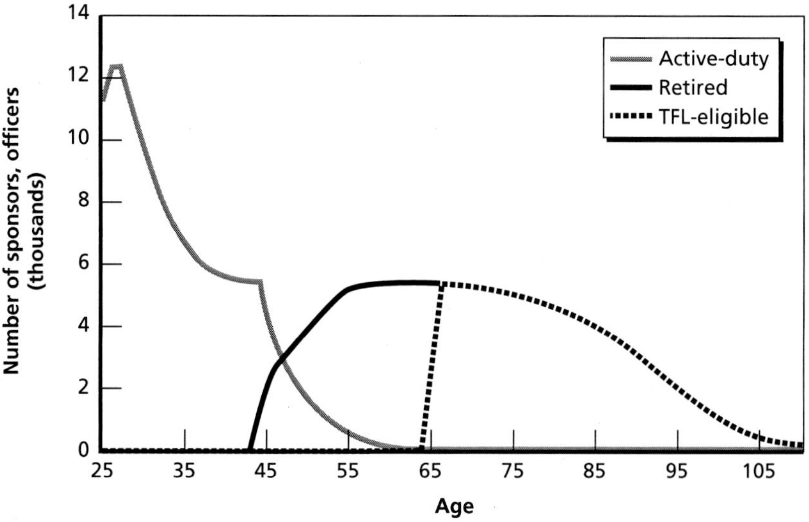

RAND *MG598-3.2*

spouses and health benefits for spouses and certain other dependents) and of the disabled population. For simplicity of computation, DoD actuaries use a steady-state projection of the population that is updated as information about changes in mortality and dependence rates, etc., become available.

The second set of variables for which projections are required relates to the programmatic specifics of military retirement and TFL benefits. Over the years, there have been certain changes in the ways that retirement benefits are computed,[10] and as these are slowly carried through the aging inventory of active-duty and retired populations, average benefit levels change and projections are adjusted accordingly. For health benefits, projections must be made for the division of claims between private providers and options for treatment in military facilities and clinics. This requires forecasting the incidence of qualifying health events for the population, as well as for the cost of providing care under various alternatives. For military personnel who retired in 2004, the average annual benefit was $26,692 for enlisted personnel and $53,179 for officers.[11] Under TFL, the average claim cost varies with age, but was in the range of $5,500 to $7,500 for those over 65 years of age in 2004. The DoD actuaries need to project numbers for a number of economic variables:

---

[10] The old formula used the pay in the last month before retirement as the benchmark, and the current formula, called High-3, takes the average of the highest paid three years of service as the benchmark; there is also a variant called REDUX which allows personnel to take a $30,000 bonus at YOS 16 in exchange for a reduction in retirement benefits. In addition, the pay tables have on occasion been tweaked to affect the economic incentives for retention beyond 20 YOS. For details, see DoD, Office of the Actuary, *Valuation of the Military Retirement System.*

[11] These are the averages for retirees with years of service ranging from 20 to 35. Enlisted retirement pay at 20 YOS was a little over $21,000; it was over $64,000 for those with 35 YOS. For officers, retirement pay ranges from $38,000 to almost $110,000. The formula for computing the retirement benefit is base pay × 2.5% × YOS, where basic pay varies depending on which retirement rule applies (see footnote 21). Staying longer usually pays off, as promotions and increased years of service raise the value of the retirement package; however, the pay table is constructed to limit the incentive to stay beyond YOS 26.

- the rate of growth in military pay (currently projected at 3.75 percent per year)
- the rate of real interest (currently projected at 3.25 percent)
- the general inflation rate (currently projected at 3.0 percent)
- the discount rate, which equals the real rate plus inflation (currently projected at 6.25 percent)
- the rate of inflation for medical benefits (currently projected at 6.25 percent).

These projections are developed by the two boards of actuaries after analysis of past data trends and comparisons to similar assumptions in other relevant federal programs and private plans. In cases where the current rate is higher or lower than the assumptions listed above, the actuaries determine a reasonable transition period for reaching the steady-state, long-term levels in the projections.

With all these data, assumptions, and projections in hand, the actuaries can compute the precise values for use in Equations 3.1 and 3.2. The normal cost percentage for retirement purposes was 31.4 percent in 2004, and the per capita normal cost for TFL accrual was $5,436. Applying these values, Figure 3.3 and Figure 3.4 illustrate the time-path of a notional trust fund for the retirement and TFL benefit programs, respectively.

When applying Equation 3.1 and 3.2 to compute the normal costs as the bases for inclusion the President's budget submission to Congress, DoD actuaries do not separate out one normal cost for each cohort in the inventory. Because their goal is to ensure that the total postretirement system of cash payments and health services for retirees is funded adequately, they compute the status of one trust fund for retirement and another for TFL benefits. However, one could also compute a separate trust fund for each new entering cohort and then aggregate these single-cohort trust funds into one common fund for the entire force. Indeed, these two methods are logically and arithmetically identical, as long as the computations use the same assumptions and projections. As it is easier to compute a single-cohort trust fund, this is what we show in the graphs above. That is, using the DoD actu-

Figure 3.3
Notional Cohort Trust Fund for Retirement Benefits

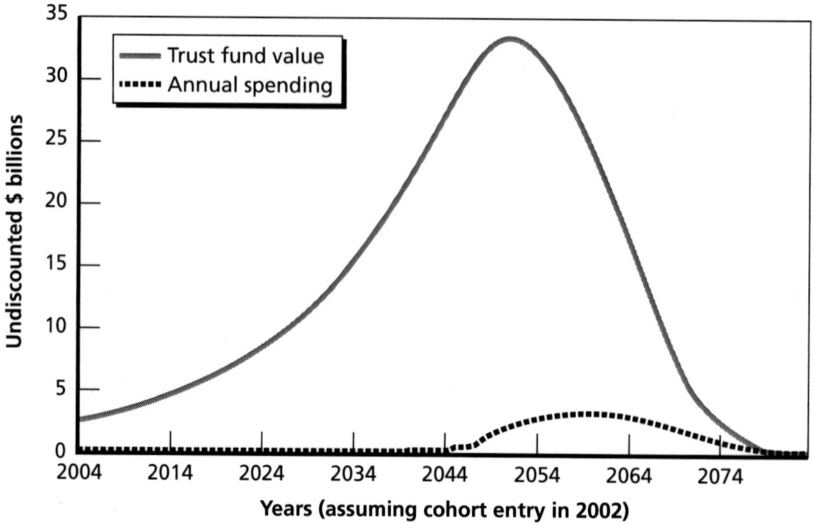

RAND *MG598-3.3*

Figure 3.4
Notional Cohort Trust Fund for TFL Benefits

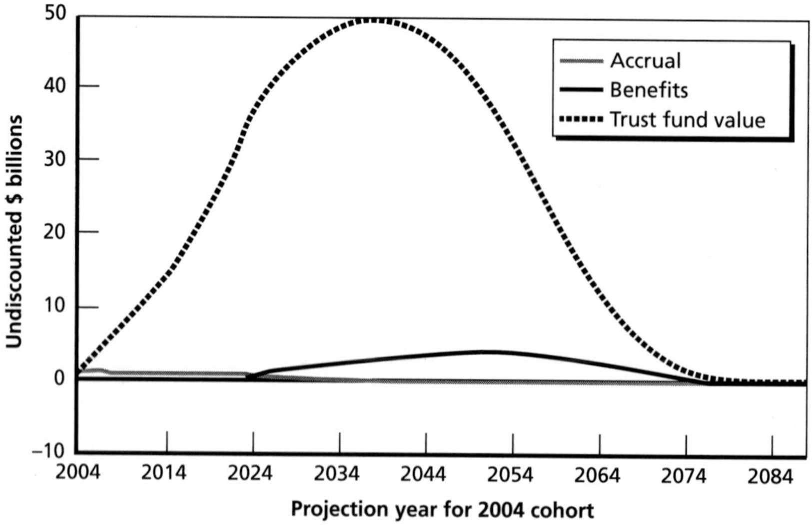

RAND *MG598-3.4*

aries' assumptions and methods, Figure 3.3 and Figure 3.4 illustrate the results of our computation of the course of the following variables:

- the collection of contributions to the trust funds, on behalf of future retirees, shown in the graphs on the horizontal axes as accrual during YOS 0–35
- the payment of benefits to eligible beneficiaries, which, in the case of retirement benefits, begin after 20 YOS (and for a limited number of personnel after less than 20 YOS), balloon up as members of the cohort reach age 65 and become eligible for Medicare, and then begin to decline until the last eligible beneficiary has passed away
- the annual net value of the trust fund assets, which is computed using the following simple arithmetic: adding DoD's annual contributions to the accrued interest paid by the Department of the Treasury on the net assets in the trust fund during the prior year and subtracting the pension and health benefits paid out.[12]

If all the actuarial assumptions and projections are correct, then the single-cohort trust fund should accumulate just the right amount of initial contributions from DoD, grow nominally with the compounded interest contributions on net assets on the books of the Department of the Treasury, and be completely exhausted at the time the last beneficiary has passed away, just as Figures 3.3. and 3.4 illustrate. The initial contributions, with accumulated interest, accrue rapidly throughout the initial years of the trust fund, the book value of which keeps growing as long as contributions and interest exceed annual payments. Once this growth peaks and annual benefit payments begin to exceed interest payments, the net value of the fund declines until it is exhausted and all benefits have been paid out. This is the essence of a defined benefit trust fund computed for a single cohort. In actual practice, there is, as mentioned, only one consolidated trust fund for all cohorts, which is never depleted; nevertheless, the concept of the AEAN method is

[12] For illustrative purposes, Figure 3.4 mixes *flows* (values paid in and out per year) with *stocks* (the point-in-time total value of the fund measured any one year).

quite consistent with the results shown above. We used the following sources, methods, and assumptions to compute the values shown in Figures 3.3 and 3.4:

- The DoD actuaries' steady-state inventory projections, applying their annual transition probabilities for officers and enlisted personnel separately to arrive at a projection of the future retention history of the entering 2004 cohort.[13]
- The DoD actuaries' projections for death rates for eligible retirees and dependents.[14]
- The 2004 DoD pay table, from which we computed grade-weighted pay by YOS for all years from 1–35.
- Projections of future pay for the personnel inventory by YOS, using the actuaries' assumptions of a 3.75 percent annual pay growth.
- For retirement benefits, we computed future retirement pay using the High-3 formula as applicable to the 2004 cohort, applied to the actuaries' projected annual retirements from YOS 20–35, using the actuaries' projected Consumer Price Index (CPI) inflation rate of 3 percent annually.
- For health benefits, we computed future benefits under TFL to be paid to primary beneficiaries, both disabled and nondisabled, and their dependents, using the actuaries' assumed medical inflation rate of 6.25 percent.
- All future pay and benefits were discounted to 2004 using a 6 percent discount factor (the sum of the CPI inflation rate and the actuaries' assumed real interest rate of 3 percent); this factor was also applied to compute the trust fund interest payments made by the Department of the Treasury.

---

[13] We made only one simplifying assumption in these projections: We assumed that all entering personnel are the same age. In reality, the age span of entering enlisted personnel is from 16 to 30, and for officers from 24 to 40. We computed weighted averages for these ages from the actuaries' data and used 21 for enlisted and 25 for officers in our calculations.

[14] We compared the actuaries' computation with the revisions to projected mortality improvement factors newly computed by Ryan Edwards in unpublished research for Queens College of the City University of New York.

We then applied the DoD actuaries' published normal costs, as computed by them using their own modeling and computations (Equations 3.1 and 3.2). For retirement accrual, the current rate used by OACT is 31.5 percent of basic pay; for TFL accrual, the per capita accrual rate is $5,436.

This basic exposition of the DoD accrual methods and the two military retirement trust funds lays the groundwork for a demonstration of the substantial problems that arise in estimating the cost of a military person-year. There are significant hurdles to overcome before the cost of postretirement benefits can be correctly rolled in to any estimate of the cost of current military person-years. Indeed, the application of DoD actuaries' normal costs to any effort to determine the cost of a military person-year (either to DoD or to the FG as a whole) will not, in fact, produce a reliable and meaningful number. Several methodological refinements must first be introduced.

Weighting Normal Cost with Retirement Probabilities

As explained in the previous section, in trust fund accrual as practiced by DoD actuaries applying the AEAN method, the retirement normal cost is a constant percentage of the military payroll for basic pay, and the TFL normal cost is a flat per capita charge for both officers and enlisted personnel. The first problem with this method of retirement accrual is that it is unrelated to the actual probability of the members of any cohort actually reaching retirement eligibility—indeed, this is one of the hallmarks of the AEAN method. Figure 3.5 illustrates this practice.

The top line in Figure 3.5 shows RMC distributed across the personnel inventory (officers and enlisted together) by YOS, with pay graded according to the average grade for each YOS. RMC is defined as the sum of base pay and benefits, and the second line from the top in the figures shows base pay. The second line from the bottom shows the DoD actuaries' normal cost for retirement accrual as a percentage of base pay (i.e., this line is a displacement of the base pay line above it). The bottom line represents accrual for TFL, which is a per capita charge

Figure 3.5
DoD Accrual Charges Are Unrelated to Retirement Probabilities

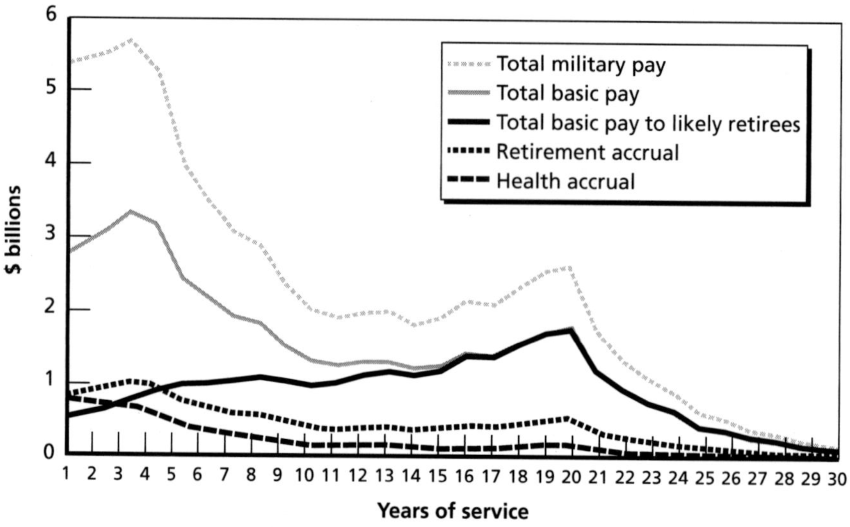

RAND *MG598-3.5*

across the entire force. Since base pay is the product of the number of people in each YOS and the annual pay rate, the line for health accrual has a shape that looks somewhat like base pay. These four lines together illustrate the fundamental nature of the AEAN methods as applied by the DoD actuaries, wherein the normal cost charges are applied uniformly across the entire inventory of personnel.

The first problem with this method is that it completely ignores the most basic fact of the military retirement system: It is a defined benefit system with zero percent vesting for personnel with less than 20 YOS and 100 percent vesting for those who have completed 20 YOS (such systems are often referred to as *cliff vesting*). Under such a system, all personnel beyond 20 YOS have already earned all the benefits they will ever receive under TFL and almost all the retirement pay to which they will be entitled. In other words, once a person has completed YOS 20, the FG is already committed to paying retirement benefits for the remainder of that person's life and the lives of any of his or her qualifying dependents. This means that the DoD actuaries' method, which assigns the same costs for retirement accrual to personnel both below and above YOS 20, is seriously misleading.[15] In reality, the only additional benefits that personnel beyond YOS 20 is due to normal pay increases (adjustments for inflation and within-grade pay increases) and to grade increases through promotion. Therefore, it is misleading to use the accrual charges levied by the actuaries in calculating the cost of a person-year for personnel beyond YOS 20—yet this is exactly how the SMCRs described above are calculated.

A second, related problem with using the AEAN method to estimate annual personnel costs is the fact that the probability of the member of a particular cohort actually reaching YOS 20 and vesting in postretirement benefits is clearly related to the number of years already served. This is shown by the cross-hatched line in Figure 3.5, which rises up to and becomes identical with the base pay line (which shows the amount of basic pay remitted to that portion of each year-group that will reach retirement) at 20 YOS. Only about 48 percent of an entering cohort of officers will ever become eligible for retirement. The corresponding number for enlisted personnel is about 16 percent, and the average for officers and enlisted personnel is about 19 percent. Obviously, as personnel stay longer in the force, they become increasingly likely to reach retirement eligibility; this illustrated in Figure 3.5 as the cross-hatched line approaches and finally becomes identical to the base pay line at YOS 20, indicating that beyond that year, all base pay is remitted to personnel who are vested in the retirement system.

Figure 3.5 shows that the two bottom lines, which indicate accrual as calculated under AEAN, are completely unrelated to the actual probability of the members of any cohort actually reaching retirement eligibility. While AEAN may be a perfectly appropriate method for computing accrual charges, it is an inappropriate method for assigning costs to different work-years, since it does not distribute the accrual costs according to the actual probabilities of personnel in any cohort actually reaching retirement eligibility.

There are two obvious ways to appropriately distribute accrual costs. The first precisely follows the letter of the military defined benefit

---

15 In fairness, this method was never designed to be used as an estimate of the cost of manpower, although that fact alone indicates that it may not be appropriate for that purpose.

plan and applies the concept of cliff vesting literally. This approach assigns zero cost for accrual and retirement benefits to all year-groups below YOS 20, based on the argument that if a military position is typically occupied by a person with less than 20 YOS, its elimination will not lead to savings in future retirement benefits, since no entitlements are earned by personnel in that position. Under the current defined benefit plan, it is YOS 20 that really costs, for personnel only earn entitlements upon completing that year. Under this method, we could assign virtually all costs of the military retirement system to YOS 20, no costs to previous years of service, and only the small, marginal increases earned for service beyond YOS 20 to personnel who stay beyond that year. This is the most literal cost interpretation of the current military retirement system.

However, such a stringent and literal interpretation of the cost of the military retirement system is inconsistent with the way the force is actually managed. In reality, the services have adopted an experiential (or statistical) basis upon which to shape the force, and it is this regular pattern that is applied in DoD actuaries' computation of accrual requirements.

Figure 3.6 shows the distribution by YOS of the statistical average of personnel in the officer corps and enlisted forces (in other words, for DoD as a whole) as computed by DoD actuaries and applied to their long-term projections. This is the weighted average of the patterns in the four military services, but similar figures could easily be shown for each of them. Figure 3.6 illustrates the traditional retention-rate pattern of personnel from YOS 1 until they leave before retirement eligibility, at YOS 20, or later (up until the statutory maximum of 35 YOS). After 11 years, about 50 percent of the officer cohort and 20 percent of the enlisted cohort remains in service. Beyond that, very few people leave before reaching retirement eligibility, as shown in Figure 3.7.

Figure 3.7 presents a clear, systematic retention-rate pattern for both officers and enlisted personnel—the closer each segment of the force gets to vesting in the retirement system, the more likely its mem-

Figure 3.6
Steady-State Personnel Inventory Used for Accrual

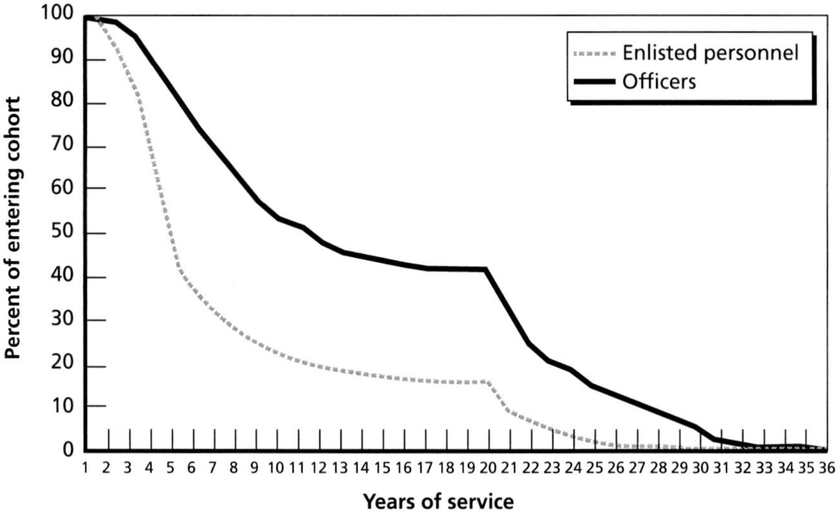

RAND *MG598-3.6*

Figure 3.7
Percentage of Personnel in Each YOS Who Will Vest in Retirement Benefits

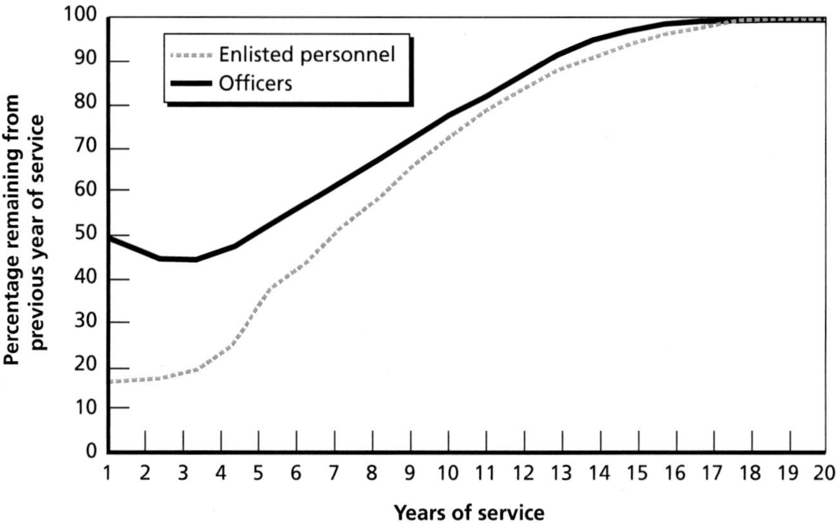

RAND *MG598-3.7*

bers are to stay. Indeed, the retention rates increase every year,[16] reaching levels above 90 percent after YOS 15. Clearly, there is a relationship between a service member's proximity to the vesting and his or her willingness to stay in the military; a relationship that is made even more apparent in Figure 3.8.

Figure 3.8 shows the percentage of the force leaving each year and even more clearly illustrates the relationship between the military retirement system and retention. These retention patterns stem from a deeply ingrained, decades-old system of military personnel management that is projected to continue for decades to come. The leave rates illustrated here provide an indication of the value of human capital in the military (i.e., the value of service members' knowledge, skills, and abilities as acquired by selection and training). For both officers

Figure 3.8
Percent of Each YOS Leaving the Force

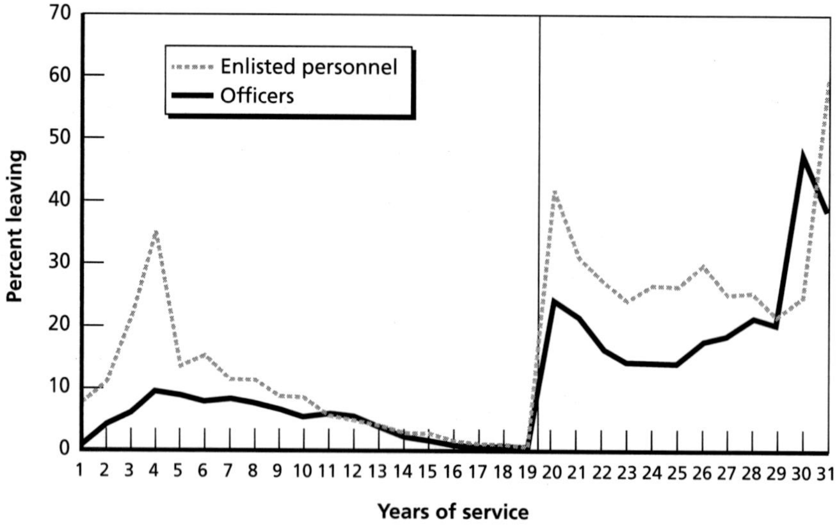

RAND *MG598-3.8*

[16] One exception to this trend occurs during the second and third year personnel are in the officer corps because of the practice of giving certain newly commissioned officers constructive credit for prior service.

and enlisted personnel, the leave rates rise in the first few years, indicating a high rate of turnover among junior military personnel, as consistent with many other professions that require a high degree of physical prowess. After that, leave rates decline up to YOS 20, reflecting the pull of the very valuable retirement package awarded at 20 YOS. Over 40 percent of the enlisted force and 25 percent of the officer corps remaining after 20 YOS leave within one year, indicating a management system that accepts that, in spite of years of investing in a cohort, the value of a significant portion of the cohort's members is less than the annual costs of retaining them. These individuals are not discouraged from exercising their right to retire. After the exodus that occurs immediately following YOS 20, the leave rates stay high, until almost all of the cohort is gone by YOS 30.[17]

Clearly, the patterns of retention in the historical data that DoD actuaries use for the steady-state projections are directly related to the military retirement system's cliff-vesting structure. The system appears to be designed to induce retention up to YOS 20 and then to induce high leave rates.[18] The cliff-vesting construct is the single most important cause in the gradual lowering of the leave rates as a cohort approaches YOS 20, and the high leave rates immediately after it reaches YOS 20.

Since the military personnel system has long been adapted to accommodate the retention patterns discussed above, it would be wrong to assign all costs of the retirement system to YOS 20 alone. Clearly, we need to recognize that view that the retirement system was deliberately constructed to induce retention and that the costs of retirement benefits should be assigned across the force. The obvious way to do that is to assign retirement costs to each YOS based on the retention patterns induced by the cliff-vesting system; in other words, the costs of accrual should be distributed in proportion to the probability of each year-

---

17 Historically, the maximum YOS allowed by law has been 35. This was recently extended to 40 YOS. Very few (and only very senior) personnel with special competencies will be affected by this changes.

18 This is yet another case in which appearances can be deceiving, since the system's designers did not actually intend to induce retention up to but not beyond YOS 20.

group actually reaching retirement eligibility. Using this methodology, the accrual costs of year-groups with small retirement probabilities will be assigned a lower cost than year-groups with high retirement probabilities. This is similar to experience rating in any standard insurance system: If the members of one pool of insured people are more likely to make claims against the insurer than the members of another pool, then the former should be charged a higher premium than the latter. Similarly, if the members of one group of employees are more likely to retire than those in another, then the first group should be assigned a higher share of the retirement costs than the second. The application of this simple principle to the costing of military person-years requires assigning total accrual costs to those with less than 20 YOS in direct proportion to each year-group's likelihood of actually vesting.

This principle clearly applies to those who have served less than 20 YOS, but how does it apply to those beyond 20 YOS? Members of cohorts with more than 20 YOS have already vested fully in the retirement system, and the FG incurred nearly the full liability for their retirement benefits at YOS 20. The only additional costs incurred by the FG for personnel who serve beyond YOS 20 arise from any increases in the basic benefits earned at YOS 20. No additional TFL benefits accrue beyond YOS 20, but there are two reasons that retirement benefits might increase. One is built into the formula: Retirement benefits equal basic pay multiplied by 2.5 percent multiplied by YOS. According to this formula, it is possible for an active-duty service member to stay at the same rank and pay and earn additional retirement benefits due to the increase in the second multiplier that comes with every additional YOS. The other source is that longer service also may mean pay increases, either within grade or through promotion to a higher grade. For personnel beyond 20 YOS, it is clearly not correct to apply the same accrual percentage charged by DoD actuaries assessing the cost of a person-year; the only additional cost incurred by the FG for these personnel is the small added cost that comes from the aforementioned possible increases in retirement pay. The cost of the basic retirement package is fully incurred by the FG at YOS 20. Figure 3.9 contrasts accrual rates computed using this method with the rates used by DoD actuaries.

Figure 3.9
Alternative Accrual Factors for Retirement Benefits

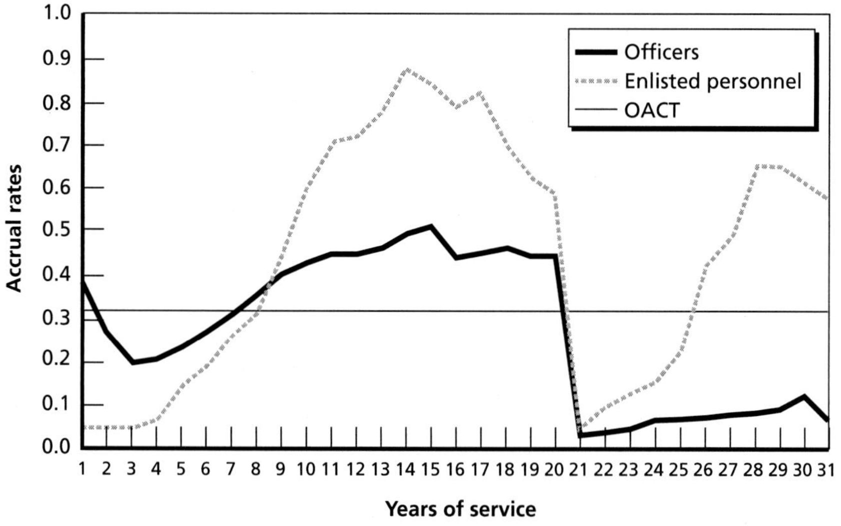

RAND *MG598-3.9*

In this figure, the solid horizontal black line represents the actuaries' average accrual rate of 31.4 percent.[19] The lines with boxes and stars represent the accrual rates that would be charged to enlisted personnel and officers, respectively, if those rates (1) were weighted according to the probability of reaching entitlement at YOS 20, and (2) only assess increases in the retirement package beyond YOS 20 weighted by the probability of serving beyond YOS 20. The average of all three lines is 31.4 percent, meaning the lines labeled *officers* and *enlisted personnel* merely represent an alternative method of spreading the same total accrual rate across the cohorts in the inventory according to the probabilities of each cohort vesting and earning additional entitlements

[19] Computed as the average accrual rate across the three retirement systems (Final Pay, High-3, and Redux), as well as the combined accrual rate for both DoD and the Department of the Treasury (which is responsible for paying accrual for the concurrent receipt benefit, a repeal of a previous reduction of military retirement benefits for retirees who also receive benefits from the DVA). See DoD, Office of the Actuary, *Valuation of the Military Retirement System*, pp. 9–11.

above the basic vested amount awarded at YOS 20. In other words, the areas under all the three curves are identical.

This raises several important points. First, this method takes as a given that the actuaries' total assessment for accrual, equal to 0.314 of the payroll for basic pay, yields the actuarially correct amount to fund all earned future benefits for current personnel. Thus, we do not make any allegation that the actuaries are assessing DoD an incorrect accrual rate. What is at issue is whether or not the actuaries' rate correctly reflects the cost of a military person-year. Under the method described here, the cost of a person-year is directly dependent on likelihood of the members of a cohort reaching retirement and of earning additional entitlement for service beyond YOS 20; it is therefore a better approach for spreading the total accrual cost across the force. The second point (which is implied by the first) is that our method assesses separate accrual rates for officers and enlisted personnel. This is a direct consequence of two facts: (1) officers have a higher probability of staying to YOS 20 than enlisted personnel have, and (2) officers have a significantly higher probability of staying beyond YOS 20 and earning additional retirement benefits than enlisted personnel have (as can be seen by inspection of the leave rates by YOS shown Figure 3.8).

These two methods for costing out a military person-year, OACT's and the method described above, yield somewhat different results. The total amounts for the entire force are the same, but they differ in how they are spread across the work-years. It is obvious that the application of a constant percentage rate for accrual means that

- younger workers look more expensive than they really are, given that very few of them will actually reach retirement eligibility
- personnel close to retirement seem less costly than they really are, given that a very high percentage of them will reach retirement eligibility
- personnel beyond YOS 20 (i.e., those who have already vested in the retirement system) appear significantly more expensive than they really are

- enlisted personnel as a group look more expensive than they really are, as a smaller proportion of them will ever vest as compared to officers.

For these reasons, using the OACT accrual rates for estimating the cost of a military person-year yields skewed and unrealistic results. As noted, either method will fund total accrual charges at the same rate; they differ only in how they assess totally charges across work-wyears. If cost is an important element in deciding which positions to civilianize, the OACT method of costing a person-year will not yield the most useful results. This is further demonstrated by applying the accrual rates shown in Figure 3.5 to the average basic pay rates, weighted by grade, as shown in Figure 3.10 and Figure 3.11.

In these two figures, we have first converted the SMCRs, which were shown above in Figure 2.1 by grade, into grade-weighted averages for each YOS (shown in the solid lines in Figure 3.10 and Figure 3.11).

Figure 3.10
Officer Retirement Accrual: Economic Compensation Versus SMCRs

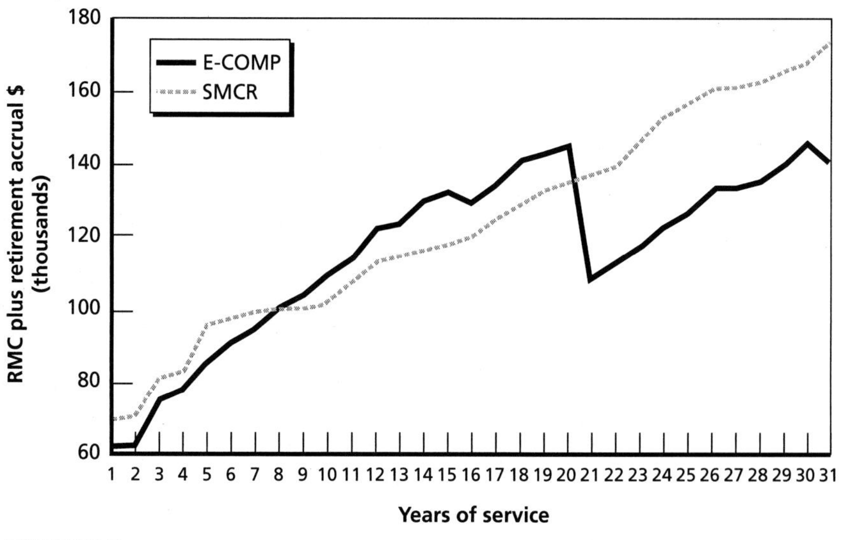

RAND *MG598-3.10*

Figure 3.11
Enlisted Retirement Accrual: Economic Compensation Versus SMCRs

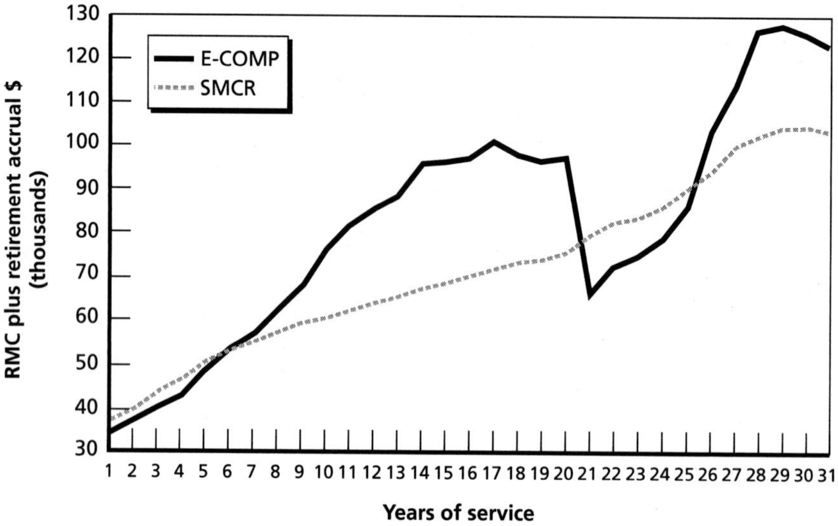

RAND *MG598-3.11*

E-COMP stands for economic compensation in both figures.[20] For the officer corps, DoD's official rates for computing gains and losses from civilianization actions overestimate the cost for young officers, understate costs of mid-grade officers, and overstate the costs for those beyond YOS 20. This general pattern also holds for enlisted personnel, the exception being that the cost of very senior NCOs beyond YOS 24 (of whom there are very few) are understated by the SMCRs. (Note that it is not appropriate to compare areas above and below the SMCR line in this figure, since they are not additive. The vertical axis represents the cost of a person-year.)

The same procedure can be used to allocate the cost of accrual for TFL across service years and cohorts. As noted above, the only difference between the two kinds of benefits is that no additional TFL benefits accrue after YOS 20. We do not show these computations here,

[20] The term E-COMP indicates that the allocation of accrual according to the method presented here is closer to the economic concept of opportunity cost (i.e., it provides a better estimate of the real cost of a person-year than the method used to compute the SMCRs).

but can make them available upon request. Instead, in Figure 3.12 and Table 3.1 we show the combined results, comparing the SMCRs with the total economic compensation rates arrived at by costing out both retirement and TFL benefits jointly.

Figure 3.12 and Table 3.1 illustrate the same data, with the table adding the ratio between the SMCR and the economic compensation amount. The SMCRs are too high for junior officers (those with 7 or less YOS), too low for officers with between 9 and 20 YOS, and much too high for officers with more than 20 YOS. The SMCRs for enlisted personnel are too high through YOS 5, much too low up for YOS 6 to YOS 20, too high between YOS 21 and 25, and then too low again through YOS 31.

Figure 3.12
Total Accrual: Economic Compensation Versus SMCRs

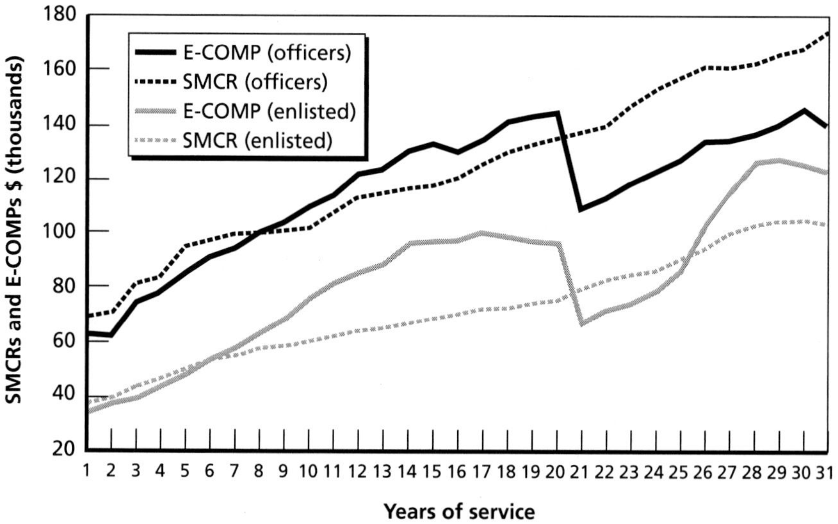

RAND *MG598-3.12*

Table 3.1
Total Accrual: Economic Compensation Versus SMCRs

YOS	Officers	SMCR (officers)	Ratio (%)	Enlisted	SMCR (enlisted)	Ratio (%)
1	$62,255	$69,226	111.2	$33,967	$36,942	108.8
2	$61,690	$70,090	113.6	$36,636	$39,502	107.8
3	$74,467	$81,612	109.6	$39,532	$43,367	109.7
4	$77,984	$83,181	106.7	$42,734	$46,375	108.5
5	$85,297	$95,260	111.7	$47,865	$49,780	104.0
6	$91,081	$97,482	107.0	$52,942	$52,772	99.7
7	$94,416	$99,242	105.1	$56,912	$54,985	96.6
8	$100,513	$99,631	99.1	$62,263	$56,868	91.3
9	$103,968	$100,190	96.4	$68,191	$58,917	86.4
10	$109,322	$101,459	92.8	$76,110	$60,339	79.3
11	$114,176	$107,441	94.1	$81,624	$61,858	75.8
12	$121,895	$113,022	92.7	$85,258	$63,620	74.6
13	$123,904	$114,647	92.5	$88,392	$64,848	73.4
14	$130,746	$116,616	89.2	$95,889	$67,114	70.0
15	$132,552	$117,613	88.7	$96,375	$68,548	71.1
16	$129,646	$120,365	92.8	$97,178	$70,249	72.3
17	$134,559	$125,326	93.1	$100,507	$71,900	71.5
18	$140,533	$128,764	91.6	$97,854	$72,857	74.5
19	$143,112	$132,415	92.5	$96,356	$73,995	76.8
20	$144,864	$134,580	92.9	$96,912	$75,184	77.6
21	$108,561	$137,016	126.2	$66,063	$79,810	120.8
22	$112,869	$139,500	123.6	$71,991	$82,424	114.5
23	$118,075	$146,876	124.4	$74,377	$83,763	112.6
24	$123,206	$152,609	123.9	$78,697	$85,922	109.2
25	$126,447	$156,834	124.0	$83,176	$90,286	108.5

Table 3.1—Continued

YOS	Officers	SMCR (officers)	Ratio (%)	Enlisted	SMCR (enlisted)	Ratio (%)
26	$133,622	$160,626	120.2	$100,748	$93,912	93.2
27	$133,194	$160,778	120.7	$112,225	$99,913	89.0
28	$135,786	$162,118	119.4	$123,844	$102,629	82.9
29	$139,300	$165,806	119.0	$124,861	$104,316	83.5
30	$145,712	$167,317	114.8	$125,210	$104,397	83.4
31	$140,180	$174,288	124.3	$114,703	$103,716	90.4

Conclusion and Implications

In this section, we have demonstrated that the Comptroller's SMCRs can be seriously misleading when used to estimate the cost of a military person-year. The reason lies in the mistaken notion that the DoD actuaries' accrual charges represent the cost of a person-year. This is a false assumption, since the real cost of a person-year depends on the probability of a person in each cohort becoming vested in the post-retirement benefit system. We have provided alternative estimates for these costs that are based on the assumption that the actuaries' accrual method provides the correct total cost of the retirement system. However, accrual should really not be counted as a cost at all, since it only represents a transfer payment within the FG. The following chapters lay out an alternative method that leads to very different estimates of the cost of a military person-year than those calculated thus far.

CHAPTER FOUR

Calculating the Correct Cost of Eliminating a Military Person-Year

In addition to the fundamental accounting errors encountered in the SMCRs, there are serious analytical shortcomings inherent in the DoD actuaries' accrual method for including the costs of postretirement benefits in estimates of the cost of a military person-year. This chapter presents a more economically sound method and shows how it can be applied to produce more accurate cost estimates.

Recomputing the Total Cost of Postretirement Benefits

The discussions in Chapters Two and Three are predicated on the assumption that the current accrual cost, however distributed across individuals in the current force, is also the correct cost of a person-year. However, this is clearly not the case, as this assumption makes the estimation of the cost of a person-year completely dependent on the particular financing scheme implemented by the FG. In fact, there are many financing schemes that could be construed as consistent with the AEAN method. The system chosen by OACT spreads the total required accrual for an entering cohort across all the future working years of that cohort; in principle, this is not a controversial procedure and would seem to be beyond criticism. The advantage of this method is that, under steady-state conditions, the accrual charge will be a constant percentage of the military payroll each year, which makes budget predictions easier (an important consideration for DoD, the Office of

Management and Budget [OMB], and Congress). Another version of funding using the AEAN method would be to assess the entire future liability for each entering cohort and then deposit that amount in the trust fund. Under this financing scheme, all costs for the actuarial projections of a cohorts future benefits would be assessed upon their entry into service, and no further contributions would be needed for that cohort. Yet another version would be to fund all liabilities for future benefits only in the year of vesting, and none before that. Under this scheme, all payments would be made in YOS 20, with some additional payments each year for those who stay beyond YOS 20. Under the first approach, payments would be spread out over the working years of the cohort; under the second, all payments would be made up front in year one; under the third, all payments would be made only in YOS 20 and beyond.

Under all of these financing schemes, the FG will pay in the total amount required for future benefits payments; they differ only with respect to when that payment is made. That is, the total cost to the FG is exactly the same in all three cases, since the benefits paid out are exactly the same. If the costs to the FG are the same under the three approaches, then, by implication, the estimated cost for a person-year should also be the same. Yet, taking the approach suggested by the SMCRs, the costs would differ vastly. In the first case (which is the method used today), the cost of a person-year is estimated by adding the annual accrual to basic pay. In the second, the cost of the first YOS is estimated to be extraordinarily high, and all subsequent work-years are costed only at the annual RMC paid to service personnel. In the second case, all years up to YOS 20 are costed at the RMC annual compensation rate, and YOS 20 shows an enormous spike in compensation costs. These three methods yield different estimates of the cost of an individual person-year, yet the cost to the FG for all person-years is exactly the same in all three cases, proving that the person-year costing method must be independent of any particular budgeting scheme. This will ensure that the estimate of the real cost of a military person-year is not confounded by essentially arbitrary choices made during the preparation of budget presentations for Congress.

When viewed in this manner, the cost estimates for postretirement benefits presented in the two previous chapters are clearly incorrect, as they are captive to a particular method for spreading accrual costs across work-years. Put another way, under the current official cost-estimating method, a person-year is burdened only with a single year's contribution to the funding of future benefits, whereas in fact it takes the entire expected working life of a retiring service member to build up sufficient contributions to pay all future benefits. Relying on the accrual method for estimating the cost of a work-year will significantly underestimate the true cost to the FG of all postretirement benefits. In fact, this method only captures between 3 and 5 percent of the total cost, since careers qualifying for postretirement benefits can extend to anywhere between 20 and 35 years and accrual is calculated as a constant percentage of pay.

Chapter Three shows that the cost of a particular person-year is related to the probability of a member of that cohort actually vesting in the retirement system at YOS 20, as well as the probability of earning additional benefits beyond that year. This chapter builds on that approach but shows how to estimate the total cost of all future benefits that are incurred by the FG from a current person-year rather than estimating the cost of only one year's accrual.

A Simple Computational Example

Take, for example, the computation of the annual person-year costs of the employees of a small company with the following characteristics:

- an initial cohort of 1,000 hires gradually declines to 350 over five years
- a starting salary of $1,000, growing at 3.75 percent per year
- a defined retirement benefit in the form of a lump sum equal to $3,000 in which all employees are fully vested after 5 YOS
- a trust fund where assets are invested at an annual rate of return of 6.25 percent.

These assumptions are illustrated in Table 4.1, along with the relevant computations for calculating the liability for the defined benefit plan.

Under these assumptions, the company will have to pay $1,050,000 at the end of year five, or $3,000 to each of the remaining 350 workers who have met the cliff-vesting eligibility retirement rules after staying for five years. Discounting the total benefits to year one at the discount rate of 6.25 percent yields a present value of total benefits of $775,434. The annual salaries per person are given in the third column of the table, and the total annual costs, discounted to year one, in column four. The total present value (TPV) of salary costs is then $2,683,204. The normal cost can be computed by applying Equation 2.1 (the ratio of the total present value of benefits to the TPV of salaries) to get a normal cost of 0.289. This calculation provides the basis for funding the company's trust fund, so as to ensure that there will be sufficient assets to pay out the defined benefits at the end of year five. Table 4.2 illustrates the three methods for accomplishing this discussed thus far.

Table 4.1
Basic Data for a Hypothetical Defined Benefit Plan

Year	Size of cohort	Annual Salary	TPV Annual Cost
1	1,000	$1,000	$941,176
2	700	$1,038	$643,322
3	500	$1,076	$448,703
4	400	$1,117	$350,517
5	350	$1,159	$299,485

Benefit: $3,000
Retirees: 350
Benefits owed: $1,050,000
Annual pay raise: 3.75%
Discount rate: 6.25%
TPV benefits: $774,434
PV total costs: $2,683,204
Normal cost: 28.9%

Table 4.2
Trust Fund Assets Under Three Alternatives

Alternative 1		Alternative 2		Alternative 3	
Annual Accrual	Trust Fund Assets	Initial Accrual	Trust Fund Assets	Final Accrual	Trust Fund Assets
$271,996	$288,995	$775,434	$823,898	N/A	$0
$197,537	$516,941	N/A	$875,392	N/A	$0
$146,389	$704,788	N/A	$930,104	N/A	$0
$121,503	$877,934	N/A	$988,235	N/A	$0
$110,302	$1,050,000	N/A	$1,050,000	$1,050,000	$1,050,000

N/A = not applicable.

Under method one, annual accrual, the appropriate normal cost percentage would be applied to the annual payroll, and that amount set aside in the trust fund. The trust fund assets would be invested at 6.25 percent and accumulate interest until withdrawn. At the end of five years, the fund would have the exact amount required to pay the benefits vested under the plan rules. Under method two, the present value of the total benefits would be deposited in the trust fund in year one, with no additional payments after that time. As in the first case, the assets would accumulate with interest, so that after five years the trust fund has precisely enough assets to pay all required benefits. Under method three, no deposits would be made into the trust fund until the end of year five; again, all benefits would be adequately funded, but only one single, last-year payment would have to be made. Obviously, each of these methods would be adequate for funding the required benefits. Although legal requirements may prevent the use of one or the other, taken together they illustrate the point that annual person-year costs will differ depending on the accrual method chosen.

Table 4.3 shows how the annual cost of a person-year can be computed using a method that is completely independent of whether or not there is a trust fund that requires any kind of accrual. This method takes into account only the cost incurred by the company and sets aside any consideration of funding future benefits for now.

As before, the present value of future benefits is calculated for each year. The second column is computed by discounting the final payment of $1,050,000 at 6.25 percent for the right number of years. The third column provides the retention rates, computed from the data on the personnel inventory in Table 4.1. This yields the probability that the members of that cohort will actually reach vesting at year five. The final column is the product of the first two; it represents the probability-weighted present value of the company's liability under the defined benefit plan. That is, the final column is the likely cost of employing the number of people on the payroll that year.

These data can then be used to compute the cost of a person-year. Table 4.4 and Figure 4.1 show the total annual costs as calculated using the four different methods divided by the annual personnel inventory.

Table 4.3
Probability-Weighted Benefit Costing Method

Year	PV Benefits by YOS	Cohort Probability of Vesting	Cohort Cost of Benefit Plan
1	$823,898	0.35	$288,364
2	$875,392	0.50	$437,696
3	$930,104	0.70	$651,073
4	$988,235	0.88	$864,706
5	$1,050,000	1.00	$1,050,000

Table 4.4
Calculating Person-Year Cost Under Four Different Methods

Year	Annual Accrual	Initial Accrual	Final Accrual	Probability-Weighted Cost
1	$1,272	$1,775	$1,000	$1,288
2	$1,320	$1,038	$1,038	$1,663
3	$1,369	$1,076	$1,076	$2,379
4	$1,421	$1,117	$1,117	$3,279
5	$1,474	$1,159	$4,159	$4,159

Figure 4.1
Calculating Person-Year Costs Under Four Different Methods

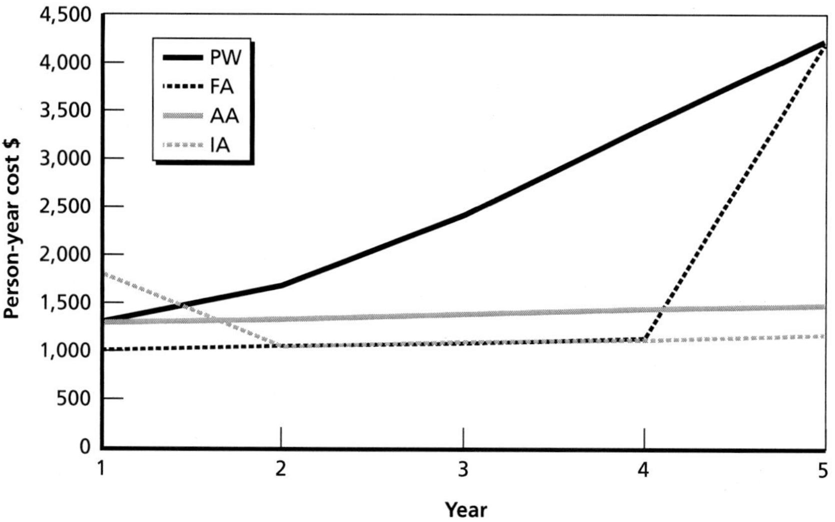

RAND *MG598-4.1*

Under initial accrual, the first-year per-person cost is higher than the per-person cost in the remaining years, and under the final accrual, the cost of the last year shoots up. Under annual accrual, the per-person cost is higher than the annual salary by the normal cost factor. As stated above, these three methods provide different estimates of the cost of a person-year depending on the accrual method chosen. This is obviously problematic, since the liability for the company is exactly the same under all three methods—it pays the same annual salaries to its personnel and provides exactly the same benefits to its retirees. Thus, all of these methods provide misleading cost estimates.

A more appropriate estimate of the cost of a person-year is shown in Table 4.4 and Figure 4.1 as probability-weighted cost. This method used to arrive at this estimate has two significant advantages. First, it is completely independent of accrual method; it will return the same results with any of the three trust fund schemes presented above, or with any combination of them. Second, it produces a much more accurate estimate of the cost of a person-year because it includes only the annual salary and the likely cost of each employee in that cohort actually retiring. The latter represents only the current likelihood of having to pay benefits to someone vesting in the defined benefit plan, which is all that is required to estimate the annual costs of the company's current employees.

Note that the probability-weighted cost-estimation method yields a significantly higher cost for a person-year than does the annual-accrual method. The bias caused by using the annual-accrual method for estimating the cost of a person-year cost is about 2 percent in the first year, 43 percent in the third year, and almost 66 percent in the fifth. Using the annual accrual method for assigning costs to a person-year will therefore yield very significant understatements of the real economic cost of someone on the payroll. In other words, the probability-weighted method uncovers the likely savings the company will receive from eliminating a position. It shows that if the company were to reduce its personnel inventory, it would not only reduce current salary payments but also reduce the likelihood of having to pay postretirement benefits at some time in the future.

The annual-accrual method currently used by DoD to asses the cost of a person-year is seriously misleading. This method only gives the savings from not having to pay salaries and avoiding one year's accrual payment; it does not indicate possible savings from entirely eliminating the need to pay future benefits to a retiree. Hence, the annual accrual method understates the true opportunity cost of employing a person who may or may not reach retirement eligibility. Dramatic results can be obtained with the probability-weighted cost assignment method is applied to the current military personnel inventory.

The Full Economic Cost of a Military Person-Year

The U.S. military retirement system is quite extraordinary in at least three regards.[1] First, it takes 20 years of active service to vest. Second,

[1] As noted above, we did not consider reservists' retirement schemes in this study, although our computations could be applied to them as well. Reservists do not receive annuities until they turn 60 years of age, and the formula for computing their benefits is different altogether, since they amass retirement points rather than YOS.

benefits begin to be paid out immediately after retirement and continue for the rest of the retiree's life (or the life of a qualifying survivor). Third, it provides for a very generous retirement income.[2]

The average grade of an officer at YOS 20 is 4.6, i.e., a little more than halfway between major and lieutenant colonel (or lieutenant commander and commander in the Navy). The average grade of an enlisted person at YOS 20 is 7.1, which is a sergeant first class in the Army, a chief petty officer in the Navy, a gunnery sergeant in the U.S. Marine Corps, and a master sergeant in the Air Force. At these grades, the average basic pay in 2004 for an officer was just over $74,000 per year; for an enlisted person, it was just about $40,000. Using the High-3 formula, in which retired pay is the average pay for the last three YOS multiplied by 2.5 percent multiplied by YOS, the average annual retirement pay at YOS 20 for a typical officer was $37,000; that for an enlisted person was $20,000. The average age of retirement for an officer is 45 years versus 41 for enlisted personnel, reflecting the fact that almost all officers are college graduates when entering the service.[3] The average age of death is 82 for officers and 79 for enlisted personnel. That is, an officer who retires after 20 YOS of service will receive $37,000 per year, adjusted for inflation every year, for an average of 37 years, and the enlisted person retiring with 20 YOS will receive $20,000 per year, adjusted for inflation every year, for an average of 38 years. However, a significant proportion of both officers and enlisted personnel continue to serve in the military beyond 20 YOS and earn additional benefits over and above the basic entitlement due to promotions or in-grade pay increases and the ever increasing YOS multiplier, and these additional benefits must be accounted for in any effort to determine the total value of the retirement benefits.

For example, consider a marathon race with the following rules. For each mile a runner completes, he or she will receive $20. If the

---

[2] The military retirement system is much more generous than the federal civilian system, for example; we will show just how much so below.

[3] The exception is that some officers enter from enlisted ranks, and not all of these individuals have a college degree. On the other hand, many career enlisted personnel complete studies for bachelors' degrees, and quite a few also attain masters' degrees, on their own personal time while also serving full time.

runner completes 20 miles, he or she will be awarded a bonus of $1,000 payable immediately upon the completion of the race. For each additional mile to the completion of the 26 mile marathon, the runner earns another $100. To compute their cost per mile for each runner, the organizers need to know the dropout rate at each mile in the race. For every runner who stops before 20 miles, the organizer pays out $20 multiplied by the number of miles the runner completed. For every runner who passes the 20 mile mark, the organizer is immediately indebted for the full $1,000. For every runner who completes additional miles beyond 20, to the full 26 miles, the organizer owes another $100 per mile. A statistical table showing the skill and endurance of runners of this can be used to compute the likely cost for each mile of the race. The number of runners likely to complete every mile of the race from 1 through 26 is simply multiplied by the payoff for the number of miles each dropout has earned to arrive at the total cost of the race. That means that the cost of someone passing the 20 mile mark is $1,000 plus the probability of completing additional miles times the payoff per mile after 20. This principle can be applied to the problem of determining the cost of a military person-year.

Using such a computation, the average cost of a person in the inventory completing 20 YOS in the military is $51,800 for an officer and $24,800 for an enlisted person. Thus, the basic entitlement at YOS 20 ($37,000 versus $20,000) must be adjusted for the likelihood of a person serving beyond YOS 20, which can be calculated based on historical retention patterns (or leave rates) for each YOS in the personnel inventory. The actual amount of money this equates to can be computed from the total present value of the annuities each person would get, in keeping with the marathon race example. If the FG were to hand out the all future retirement income as a single bonus check immediately upon an individual's retirement (like the prize money in the marathon example above), how much would DoD have to pay out to each retiree?

Computing the lump-sum equivalent of an annuity requires four more assumptions, the first two of which are the expected life span of the retiree (currently 82 years of age for officers and 79 for enlisted personnel) and the value of the initial annuity (as indicated earlier,

$37,000 for an officer and $20,000 for an enlisted person). The next is the annual increase in the retirement paycheck, which by law is adjusted for increases in the CPI (as before, for our purposes we assume this to be 3 percent). The last assumption needed is the discount rate (we use 6.25 percent, which is the sum of the inflation rate and the real rate of interest). This is also the expected rate of return on investments. These assumptions can be applied to the standard formula for an annuity:

$$PV_a = C_n \frac{1 - \frac{1}{(1+d)^n}}{d} \tag{4.1}$$

$$C_n = A_{n=1}(1+i)^n \tag{4.2}$$

Here, C is the annuity, which grows by the inflation rate i; d is the discount rate; and n is the number of periods of the payout. Applying this formula, the present value of an officer's entitlement at YOS 20 comes to $1,049,337, and that of an enlisted person to $564,154. This means that if a person who retired at YOS 20 were given a lump-sum payment of these respective amounts, invested them in securities earning 6.25 percent per year, and withdrew an annual payment equal to the initial value of $37,000 for an officer and $20,000 for an enlisted person, then the entire amount awarded would be totally exhausted at age 82 for an officer and age 79 for an enlisted person. This is not to suggest that the retirement system should be replaced with lump-sum payments; these calculations are merely intended to determine the present value of the cost of the military retirement system to the FG.

This means that the cost to the FG of an average person retiring at YOS 20 in FY 2004 was just over a million dollars per officer, and well over half a million per enlisted person. However, these figures must be adjusted to account for the likelihood of service members staying beyond 20 YOS. This calculation is performed exactly as before, using the values of average compensation at $51,800 for an officer and $24,800 for an enlisted person. The present value lump sum equivalents of these amounts are $1,470,000 and $697,000, respectively. That is to say, on average, each officer who completes 20 YOS costs the FG almost a million and a half dollars, and the average enlisted person costs just about $700,000. These costs must now be adjusted to account for the probability of each person in each year-group of the inventory actually reaching retirement eligibility.

This computation can be performed using exactly the same assumptions and approach, the only difference being the addition of a projection of the retirement pattern of the current entry cohort (i.e., all values need to be inflated through the retirement ages of each cohort currently in the inventory). These calculations proceed using the following assumptions:

- Data on the current inventory and the pay table by grade and YOS are taken from the *Green Book*, published by the Office of the Under Secretary of Defense for Personnel and Readiness.[4]
- Retention and retirement projections come from the actuaries' steady state values published in the annual Valuation of the Retirement System.
- Mortality factors for retirees are taken from the same source.
- The assumptions regarding inflation (3 percent) and discount factor (6.25 percent) are those used by DoD actuaries.[5]
- The assumption for the annual growth rate of military pay is also the same as the DoD actuaries', at 3.75 percent.

---

[4] U.S. Department of Defense, Office of the Under Secretary for Personnel and Readiness, Directorate of Compensation, *Selected Military Compensation Tables*, also known as the *Green Book*, January 1, 2006.

[5] Federal agencies are bound by rules promulgated by OMB regarding what discount rates to use. However, since the two boards of actuaries are federal advisory boards, charged with making the best actuarial estimates available, they do not follow these rules. In fact, the discount rates are different for retirement and for health—the former uses 6 percent and the latter 6.25 percent (the rate we used here).

The computational procedure is straightforward from this point on. The numbers of personnel who will reach retirement eligibility at YOS 20 and how many of them will stay beyond YOS 20 are projected from the size of the entry cohort. The future basic pay for all likely retirees from the entry cohort is projected from the current pay table. The initial entitlement for a retired person is computed using the High-3 retirement pay formula. This value is then projected for the entire life span of the retiring cohort at the assumed inflation rate of 3 percent. All future payments are discounted back to the present year. That amount is then adjusted for the likelihood that members of the entry cohort will actually retire (about 48 percent for officers and about 16 percent for enlisted personnel).

The same computations are then performed for each of the cohorts in the current inventory. For each year-group, the result is the present value of its retirement annuities, discounted to each appropriate year in the inventory (someone in YOS 15 will retire ten years earlier than someone in YOS 5) and adjusted for the probability that the members of each year-group will reach YOS 20 and that some will also serve beyond YOS 20.

At this point, it may be helpful to illustrate the difference between the SMCRs and the economic approach in two simple formulas:

$$SMCR_t = (RMC_t + r_t)\text{basic pay}_t \tag{4.3}$$

$$EC_t = (RMC_t + \pi_t)PV(B)_t \tag{4.4}$$

Equation 4.3 states that the SMCRs are just the sum of RMC and basic pay times the accrual factor, all measured at year *t*. Equation 4.4 states that our initial estimate of the savings caused by the elimination of a billet in one year is the RMC for that year plus the present discounted value of future postretirement benefits, adjusted for the probability π that a person in that year-group will stay long enough to become entitled to these benefits. This is only a first approximation: Further refinements will be added later.

The result of all these calculations is the lump sum equivalent, in present value terms, of all future retirement annuities for each year-group in the current inventory, adjusted for the likelihood of each year-group retiring at somewhere between YOS 20 and YOS 35. Figure 4.2 and Table 4.5 show the results of these computations.

Here the capitalized values increase by YOS up to YOS 20 and then take the now-familiar sharp dip that accounts for those who have already vested in the retirement system at YOS 20. The increases up to YOS 20 are due to two factors: (1) all values are discounted one year less, reflecting the fact that the cohort in each increasing YOS has one less year to go to retirement, and (2) the probability of actually vesting increases uniformly (except for the first two years for officers, as noted above). After YOS 20, only additional benefits earned beyond the basic entitlement at YOS 20 are included, since the FG is already liable for vested benefits and these are therefore not recoverable.

The sums involved for each year are obviously significant. They should be interpreted as estimates of the financial commitment the

Figure 4.2
Probability-Adjusted Present Values of Retirement Benefits for Current Members by YOS

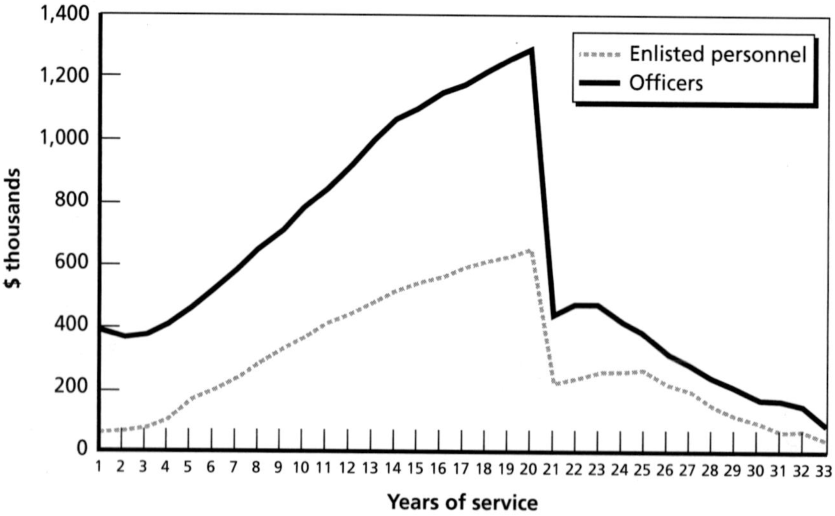

RAND *MG598-4.2*

Table 4.5
Probability-Adjusted Present Values of Retirement Benefits for Current Members by YOS

YOS	Officers	Enlisted Personnel
1	$392,276	$64,848
2	$367,838	$71,832
3	$375,057	$82,742
4	$410,121	$108,521
5	$463,890	$171,635
6	$519,819	$202,220
7	$577,073	$244,263
8	$645,746	$282,879
9	$714,260	$326,823
10	$781,648	$366,711
11	$844,312	$410,745
12	$921,487	$444,875
13	$995,056	$478,679
14	$1,054,688	$510,340
15	$1,101,886	$537,372
16	$1,144,783	$565,306
17	$1,182,646	$588,663
18	$1,218,712	$610,028
19	$1,253,145	$630,089
20	$1,285,001	$648,089
21	$440,641	$224,621
22	$471,102	$245,129
23	$465,865	$259,316

Table 4.5—Continued

YOS	Officers	Enlisted Personnel
24	$424,072	$256,960
25	$379,265	$268,230
26	$317,349	$223,785
27	$276,640	$197,325
28	$238,015	$154,487
29	$212,685	$125,290
30	$173,104	$102,744
31	$174,257	$71,464
32	$150,339	$73,283
33	$87,567	$46,147

FG undertakes when retaining the services of a military person for that year, under the crucial assumption that current personnel management practices do not change. Note what this means: If a military authorization were eliminated, the FG has only probabilistic knowledge of whether the person just removed from that position would actually reach retirement eligibility or not. In that sense, the inventory by YOS is not really managed by DoD. Retention for officers is overwhelmingly voluntary—except for a small number of persons who are not promoted after a maximum time in grade, retention decisions are made by the members of the officer corps themselves. The same is true for those enlisted personnel in the so-called career force, which generally can be said to begin with the completion of the second reenlistment at eight years. Under this personnel system, only entry into the career force is really managed by the services; once in the career force, a service member in good standing will leave only when he or she decides to.

Therefore, DoD can only know probabilistically the likelihood of a person in an authorized billet that is being considered for civilianization staying to YOS 20. Under these assumptions, the numbers in

Figure 4.2 and Table 4.5 show the total savings in terms of retirement benefits that will not have to be paid out if a position were civilianized. Therefore, they also represent the full retirement cost of keeping a person in that position for that YOS—a simple application of the economic notion of opportunity cost (i.e., the value foregone by taking a particular action). By retaining a person for each particular YOS in the table, the DoD probabilistically encumbers the FG with the full amount for that year, given currently established retention and personnel management practices. This is why we refer to these numbers as the full economic cost of the retirement system.

Note that these values should not necessarily be interpreted from the potential beneficiaries' point of view, because they do not represent the value of vesting to the military personnel in today's inventory. There are two reasons for this. First, these calculations use the DoD actuaries' health accrual discount rate of 6.25 percent. This rate is based on OACT's projections of the average long-term rate of return on real assets, such as the stock market; obviously, this may not be the appropriate subjective discount rate for any one individual.[6] Second, the values in the table and figure have been weighted by the average probability of a cohort member reaching retirement vesting—an appropriate point of view for DoD, as just noted. But no individual is average, and as retention is really voluntary on the part of military personnel (as noted in the discussion of the different notions of opportunity costs in Chapter One). For those who know that they will not remain in the military long enough to become eligible for to retirement, the retirement package obviously has no value whatsoever; for those who definitely know that they will stay to retirement, barring some chance occurrence that would force them to leave prematurely, the value of retirement benefits will exceed that indicated in the table. For each individual, only subjectively determined discount rates and retention

---

[6] Experience from the buyout schemes instituted during the DoD drawdown of military personnel in the early 1990s indicates that many military personnel have extraordinarily high discount rates. See John T. Warner and Saul Pleeter, "The Personal Discount Rate: Evidence from Military Downsizing Programs," *American Economic Review*, Vol. 91, No. 1, March 2001, pp. 33–53.

probabilities should be used to evaluate the value of prospective retirement benefits.

Next, cost of the TFL benefit must be computed; this can be done using identical calculations. As has been noted above, TFL is a program that provides benefits to Medicare-eligible retirees and their dependents. It differs from the retirement benefit in two important aspects. First, for the vast majority of retirees, TFL benefits do not become available until the retiree turns 65 and enrolls in Medicare Part B; the TFL benefits considered here do not materialize immediately upon retirement, as the retirement benefits do.[7] Second, TFL is a benefit that is not tied to income, as retirement benefits are. All TFL benefits vest at YOS 20, and no further benefits are afforded those who stay beyond YOS 20. This makes the computations a little easier, as they can neglect retention rates beyond YOS 20.

There is one other significant difference between the TFL benefit and the retirement benefit: The initial value of the retirement benefit grows over time at the assumed rate of increase of military compensation, which is set at 3.75 percent per year in the OACT projections. The cost of the medical benefit increases much more rapidly, however. According to the DoD actuaries' assumptions, the ultimate growth rate is a 6.25 percent per annum (i.e., it is identical to the discount rate). This has a significant effect on the value of the benefit: The value of the retirement-pay package grows by the wage growth for the initial payment, and then by the inflation rate for the remainder of the retiree's lifetime. The value of the TFL medical benefit grows at more than twice the rate of the inflation adjustment to the retirement benefit. Over time, this means that an ever-increasing share of the total retirement package for a retiree will consist of medical benefits.

---

[7] Under current practice, it is possible for a retiree to participate in the regular TRICARE program by paying into it. This provides access to subsidized care between retirement and becoming eligible for Medicare at age 65. We did not include the value of this benefit in our computations, since we did not have any reliable data for the usage rates and costs for this particular benefit. Therefore, the estimates that we developed are undervalued because of the unknown magnitude of the complete package of postretirement health services available to military retirees. All TRICARE benefits should be included in any final estimates; further work and data are required to accomplish this.

Estimating the present value of the TFL benefit for future cohorts requires all available cost data on the benefits payable under the program; this is then used to perform exactly the same computations as explained above for the retirement-pay benefit. Figure 4.3 and Table 4.6 show the present value of the TFL benefits to the primary sponsor, the military retiree, and all eligible dependents, computed using data provided by the DoD actuaries.

Under the current accrual practices established by the Health Board of Actuaries, the same accrual rate is used for officers and enlisted personnel on the assumption that the entitlement is the same for both. However, as the Figure 4.3 and Table 4.6 show, this is not really the case. There are certain differences in health outcomes for enlisted personnel and officers, as well as in the disability rates and dependency rates. A very important difference also lies in the age differences between the two categories. As already noted, enlisted personnel retire at an earlier age

Figure 4.3
Probability-Adjusted Present Values of TFL Benefits for Current Members by YOS

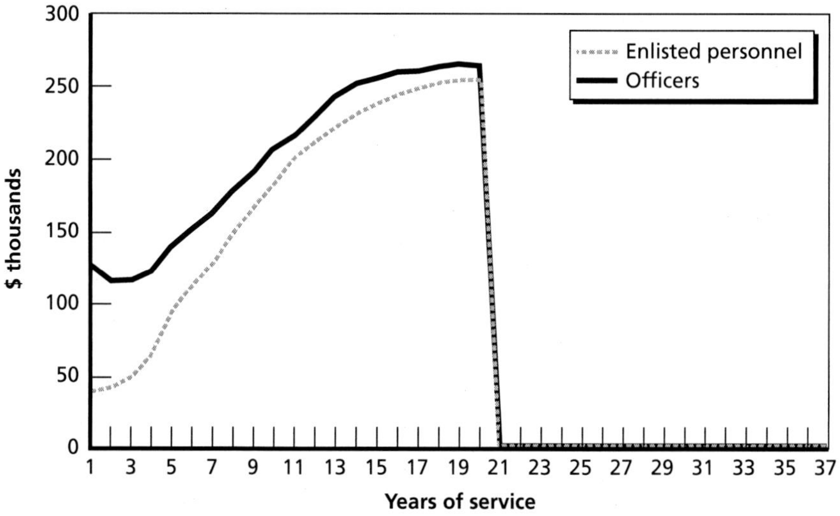

RAND *MG598-4.3*

Table 4.6
Probability-Adjusted Present Values of TFL Benefits for Current Members by YOS

YOS	Officers	Enlisted Personnel
1	$127,230	$39,953
2	$116,497	$43,214
3	$115,988	$48,606
4	$123,848	$62,250
5	$136,789	$96,138
6	$149,674	$110,604
7	$162,250	$130,456
8	$177,286	$147,525
9	$191,482	$166,432
10	$204,617	$182,350
11	$215,821	$199,440
12	$230,006	$210,930
13	$242,525	$221,618
14	$251,010	$230,717
15	$256,073	$237,221
16	$259,782	$243,681
17	$262,059	$247,778
18	$263,697	$250,730
19	$264,768	$252,881
20	$265,110	$253,985
21–35	$0	$0

than officers, on average 41 versus 45 years, which leads to a longer waiting period (and therefore to more discounting of future benefits). This lowers the present value of benefits for the enlisted personnel.

Also, the expected life span of enlisted personnel is shorter than that of officers (79 years versus 82 years), which also lowers the present value of future benefits. On average, enlisted personnel receive three year's less health benefits than officers. These are the reasons why the TFL benefit is not the same for the two categories of service personnel.

All of this information can now be pulled together into a final estimate of the cost of a military person-year to the FG. We have presented a new method for estimating the costs of the retirement benefit and the TFL benefit and have shown that the accrual method currently used by DoD underestimates the annual cost of retaining a military service member. Table 4.7 shows the results of adding up the cost estimates produced by our new method and including RMC, the regular compensation element.

These numbers are significantly higher than past estimates.[8] The weighted average across all YOS is just about $950,000 for an officer and just over $380,000 for an enlisted person. We will discuss the application of these values to civilianization decisions in Chapter Five. Briefly, the numbers state the maximum total cost avoidance that the FG can achieve by eliminating a person-year for the indicated YOS; this is the maximum gross savings from a civilianization or career termination decision.

There are a number of considerations that must be taken into account before deciding to terminate military careers at an earlier point than under past and current practices. First, since the cliff vesting of retirement benefits would force personnel to leave without any accrued benefits, it is common practice that most civilianization decisions that involve forced military career terminations offer some kind of buyout or compensation, typically at a much lower level than what the actuarially fair estimates of the loss of future benefits would be (as shown in Table 4.7). Second, it is very likely that career termination decisions will affect the management of careers and assignments for future year-

---

8 As we have noted above, past estimates of military manpower costs have only considered annual budget outlays by DoD. Table 4.7 gives estimates of the probabilistic total cost to the FG of retaining a service person on the payroll. By not including the present cost of future outlays, past estimates have been misleading.

Table 4.7
Total FG Cost of a Military Person-Year by YOS, Adjusted for Retirement Probabilities

	Officers				Enlisted Personnel			
YOS	RMC ($)	Retirement Benefits ($, PV)	TFL Benefits ($, PV)	Total ($)	RMC ($)	Retirement Benefits ($, PV)	TFL Benefits ($, PV)	Total ($)
1	46,559	392,276	127,230	566,065	31,232	64,848	39,953	136,033
2	49,161	367,838	116,497	533,496	33,611	71,832	43,214	148,657
3	62,248	375,057	115,988	553,293	36,064	82,742	48,606	167,412
4	64,731	410,121	123,848	598,700	38,089	108,521	62,250	208,861
5	69,603	463,890	136,789	670,281	39,645	171,635	96,138	307,418
6	72,647	519,819	149,674	742,140	42,524	202,220	110,604	355,347
7	73,235	577,073	162,250	812,558	43,620	244,263	130,456	418,339
8	75,773	645,746	177,286	898,805	46,122	282,879	147,525	476,526
9	76,026	714,260	191,482	981,769	47,230	326,823	166,432	540,484
10	78,549	781,648	204,617	1,064,814	49,021	366,711	182,350	598,082
11	81,149	844,312	215,821	1,141,281	49,783	410,745	199,440	659,968
12	86,491	921,487	230,006	1,237,984	51,472	444,875	210,930	707,277
13	87,119	995,056	242,525	1,324,699	52,117	478,679	221,618	752,414

Table 4.7—Continued

	Officers				Enlisted Personnel			
YOS	RMC ($)	Retirement Benefits ($, PV)	TFL Benefits ($, PV)	Total ($)	RMC ($)	Retirement Benefits ($, PV)	TFL Benefits ($, PV)	Total ($)
14	90,210	1,054,688	251,010	1,395,909	54,253	510,340	230,717	795,310
15	90,702	1,101,886	256,073	1,448,660	55,104	537,372	237,221	829,696
16	92,085	1,144,783	259,782	1,496,650	56,589	565,306	243,681	865,576
17	95,244	1,182,646	262,059	1,539,950	57,596	588,663	247,778	894,038
18	99,182	1,218,712	263,697	1,581,591	58,802	610,028	250,730	919,560
19	101,886	1,253,145	264,768	1,619,799	59,550	630,089	252,881	942,520
20	103,190	1,285,001	265,110	1,653,302	60,743	648,089	253,985	962,818
21	106,076	440,641	0	546,717	63,967	224,621	0	288,588
22	109,556	471,102	0	580,658	67,589	245,129	0	312,718
23	113,660	465,865	0	579,526	68,463	259,316	0	327,779
24	117,768	424,072	0	541,841	71,319	256,960	0	328,279
25	120,637	379,265	0	499,902	74,263	268,230	0	342,493
26	126,008	317,349	0	443,357	79,959	223,785	0	303,744

Table 4.7—Continued

	Officers				Enlisted Personnel			
YOS	RMC ($)	Retirement Benefits ($, PV)	TFL Benefits ($, PV)	Total ($)	RMC ($)	Retirement Benefits ($, PV)	TFL Benefits ($, PV)	Total ($)
27	126,489	276,640	0	403,128	84,162	197,325	0	281,487
28	127,964	238,015	0	365,980	86,116	154,487	0	240,604
29	131,217	212,685	0	343,902	87,191	125,290	0	212,481
30	133,093	173,104	0	306,197	87,220	102,744	0	189,965
31	133,093	174,257	0	307,350	87,220	71,464	0	158,684

groups below the point at which terminations are made. Third, future cohorts may come to view their career prospects differently, which may lead to changes in retention behaviors and cause problems in filling some billets. Fourth, in the case of civilianizations, there will be a cost associated with hiring a civilian replacement. These and other important considerations affect the net savings from a career termination or civilianization decision. Since these adjustment never follow any standard pattern, it is impossible to provide a table of net savings; we will have to be content with the estimates of gross savings provided in Table 4.7.

Finally, the values in the Table 4.7 have the advantage of not depending on how current payments for future retirement benefits are accumulated. The method used to calculate these figures is entirely independent of any particular method for retirement accrual. Table 4.7 shows the gross total amounts that would be saved in a terminal year if a position is eliminated (without consideration for the various adjustment issues discussed in the preceding paragraph); if the elimination involves several remaining consecutive work-years, the savings would be even greater, as we shall see when we apply the calculus in Chapter Five.[9]

Using data on the grade distribution by YOS, the data in Table 4.7 can be converted into estimates of costs by grade, illustrated in Figure 4.4. Since enlisted personnel are generally paid much less than officers with the same years of service, it is interesting to note that the cost of an E-8 is quite close to the cost of an O-6, and the cost of an E-9 close to the costs of general/flag officers. This is because the distribution of YOS for a given grade is much greater for the enlisted force than for the officer corps (and there are significant numbers of E-8s and E-9s below 20 YOS). Since they have not yet vested, but will do so with high probability, they drive the average up quite high. A much smaller proportion of O-6s and virtually no general/flag officers haveless than 20 YOS, so they have passed the threshold for cliff vesting, making their person-year cost to the FG much lower.

---

9 Table 4.7 uses data for the entire force and does not take account of the fact that reductions and drawdowns are not made uniformly across occupations. When particular occupations or career fields are chosen for culling through force reductions, the values in the table will need to be amended to reflect occupation-specific retention rates, since these may vary significantly across the force.

Figure 4.4
Probability-Weighted Costs by Grade, Officers and Enlisted Personnel

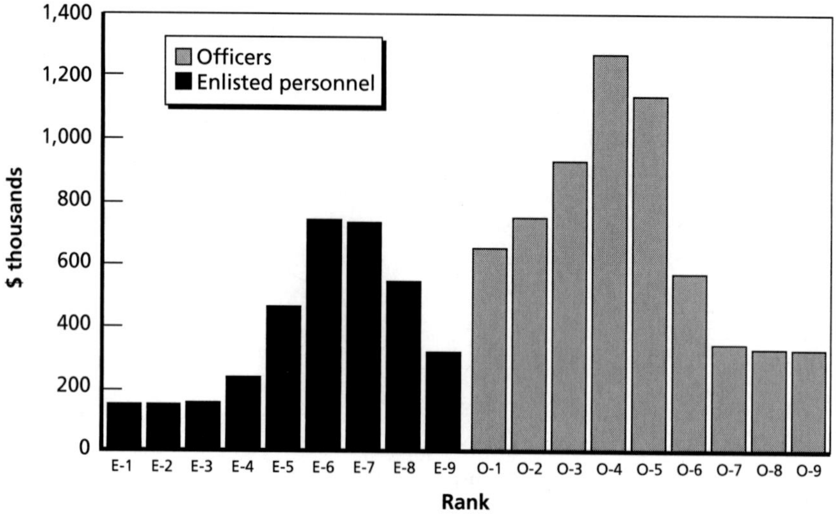

RAND *MG598-4.4*

In conclusion, we note that the closer someone gets to the magic YOS 20, the greater the cost avoidance would be should DoD eliminate their position. At these costs, it seems that if all the military positions that could be manned by civilians were civilianized, huge savings would be possible. These savings have been obscured by the present system of accounting for retirement benefits through the AEAN accrual method, the important implications of which we will discuss in Chapter Five. For now, it suffices to note that the huge differences in the cost estimates per person-year presented in this chapter, as compared to the official SMCRs reported above, are due to the application of a costing methodology that does not confound the analysis with accrual or trust fund adequacy. Although important issues in and of themselves, they have absolutely nothing to do with the costing of a military person-year. The analysis presented in this chapter demonstrates the importance of calculating the costs of the benefits, in probability-adjusted present values, and of keeping this analysis completely separate from the funding mechanism: Costs should never be confused with funding.

CHAPTER FIVE

Applying the Calculus

This chapter delves into the relationship between civilianization, which is a policy directed at military authorizations, and the two other pillars of human capital management: the personnel and compensation systems. It illustrates the complexities that can arise in seemingly simple civilianizations and the limits current budget rules place on the ability to capitalize on the present potential for significant savings through civilianization. Finally, this chapter presents a method for overcoming this weakness in the budget accounting system.

Policy and the Military-Civilian Balance in DoD

As noted in Chapter One, it has long been the official policy of DoD that only those jobs which absolutely must be performed by personnel in uniform should be staffed by military personnel; the rest should be civilian.[1] The fundamental presumption is that all tasks should be performed by civilians with the exceptions of those that cannot be performed by civilians. The latter are tasks that require specialized military training and knowledge, a military command and control structure, and control under the Uniformed Code of Military Justice. That is, the civilian workforce should, in principle, be sized first, after a care-

[1] See DoD, "Guidance for Determining Workforce Mix." The presumption that commercial activities may be more efficient than government activities led to the implementation of the A-76 process, in which government and commercial sources bid competitively for the right to perform various functions.

ful scrubbing of all positions in the services, and only then should the manpower requirement for military personnel be estimated.

Another fundamental pillar of DoD's personnel management principles is the belief that manpower authorizations are the first and most fundamental step in sizing and assigning military personnel to positions. This means that it is the responsibility of manpower communities in each of the military services to assess constantly the need for all positions in field units, commands, and support organizations. When these requirements have been scrubbed, it is up to the personnel system to hire and assign the right people to the right jobs and to create a structured sequence of assignments that will ensure the right qualifications and experience in each of the many and varied military career fields.

Every organization working within or for DoD, including any private corporations or hiring entities, should have a compensation system that is both cost-effective and sufficient to attract and retain a quality workforce. Compensation is typically divided into current compensation (cash and benefits) and deferred compensation (postretirement benefits).

DoD has long based its personnel policies on the theory that a chain of decisions is required to properly determine manpower requirements, assign and manage personnel, and structure compensation packages.[2] First, based on the operational requirements of warfighting and training, a unit structure should be created in each service with all manpower positions carefully vetted for essentiality and cost-effectiveness. Second, the personnel system has to adapt to the existing unit structure and authorized positions; not an easy task, given the many legislative imperatives and historical practices surrounding today's complicated assignment and promotion system. Add to that the fact that the current system strives to create meaningful careers, not just to fill jobs in units and commands. Third, once the tasks that need to be done and the personnel required to perform them have been identified, the compensation system should enable the personnel system to perform its tasks properly.

---

2 See DoD, "Guidance for Determining Workforce Mix."

While these are all very sound principles, they are difficult to follow in practice. With the number of different jobs and tasks in the military, a careful, continuous scrubbing of all positions based on proper industrial engineering techniques is simply not possible.[3] Therefore, a process similar to that used to construct the defense budget has gradually emerged for the development of military manpower requirements. The Secretary of Defense announces overall manpower authorizations ceilings for each of the services, along with an overall dollar limit on the total budget allocation for each service. Then, each service somehow develops operational, training, and manpower requirements that conform to these top-level budget constraints. Since requirements are built from the ground up (from units up through major commands to the service-level budget), it is usually the case that all requirements, either for manpower or functional activities, can be funded within the budgets allotted to the services. The DoD budget process is constructed to evince more demands for both manpower and funds than budget ceilings provide.

Under these circumstances, it is not surprising that senior DoD managers are not convinced that all military positions authorized are really required, and various Secretaries of Defense have issued a series of progressively more aggressive instructions to the services regarding the increased civilianization of military positions. There is an engrained conviction among the senior civilian leadership of DoD, independent of Presidential administrations, that the manpower system has allowed many positions that could be civilian to remain military. Also, on the basis of sometimes sketchy and incomplete data, it has often been alleged that the main purpose of civilianization is to save personnel costs. After all, civilian personnel cost much less than military, so there are strong cost-efficiency reasons for pursuing civilianization aggressively as general policy guidance.[4]

---

[3] It even seems that the ability to perform serious industrial engineering analyses has declined. During the military drawdown of the 1990s, many of these positions were eliminated because they were considered to be less important than others.

[4] On the basis of a recent report (GAO, *Military Personnel*), in 2005 Secretary of Defense Donald Rumsfeld lashed out at the services on this very issue, saying that he believed DoD can hire civilians at a rate that is half the cost of that of a military person.

There are many possible reasons that the pursuit of the civilianization of military positions has been less aggressive than a succession of senior leaders envisioned. In addition to a budget process that does not allow for the careful scrubbing of every position with a view toward cost-effectiveness, there is little real incentive for the services to civilianize. Unlike the President of a major corporation, the Secretary of Defense is limited to announcing guidance (either as general policy or as part of the budget process) and to using his power over final inclusions in the President's budget submission to Congress to ensure that policies are followed. These are very blunt management tools and therefore important powers over how requirements are justified. However, budgets are built and executed within the military services. Without compelling budgetary and financial incentives for pursuing civilianization, there is little reason to believe that the services will civilianize many additional positions. While the principles behind DoD civilianization policies may be sound (there may indeed be cost efficiencies to be gained from civilianizations), the policies are subject to failure unless and until the services believe that it is in their interest to execute the guidance. We will return to this issue in Chapter Six.

All of this leads to two conclusions. First, the civilianization of military positions is not, strictly speaking, a personnel policy. Effective civilianization efforts must be driven by the authorization system and come as a result of deliberate efforts to validate positions as military essential based on a set of well-defined criteria. Under such a policy, personnel managers would undertake whatever actions are required to manage to major changes in requirements. Large-scale civilianizations may also require changes in civilian pay scales. As a matter of policy, civilianization will never fully succeed if it is constrained by established personnel management principles or forced to function within the existing compensation system. Civilianization policies may be intended to influence the manpower requirements process, but policy makers must ensure that the personnel and compensation systems are able to accommodate the implementation of these policies.

This discussion of the nature of civilianization leads to the second conclusion: cliff vesting in the current military compensation system shapes retention patterns, which, in turn, forces the personnel system to adapt over time to these statistically and historically very predictable retention rates. The authorization system must then adapt to the existing inventory of career force personnel. In other words, the current system has turned causation completely on its head. As explained above, the process should move from requirements to personnel to compensation, not the other way around.

The role that the compensation system plays in shaping the force made evident in Figures 5.1, 5.2, and 5.3. DoD's budget processes are based on the presumption that requirements are first established and that funding decisions then flow from those requirements. As already noted, in practice, budgets are typically set first, and requirements are made fit them. This is true also in the personnel system, in which deferred compensation is a huge component of total compensation. Also, as previously mentioned, the military services rely on historical and statistical projections of retention rates in the career force for sizing the entry cohorts. That is to say, the services have, over time, adapted

Figure 5.1
YOS by Grade, Enlisted Force

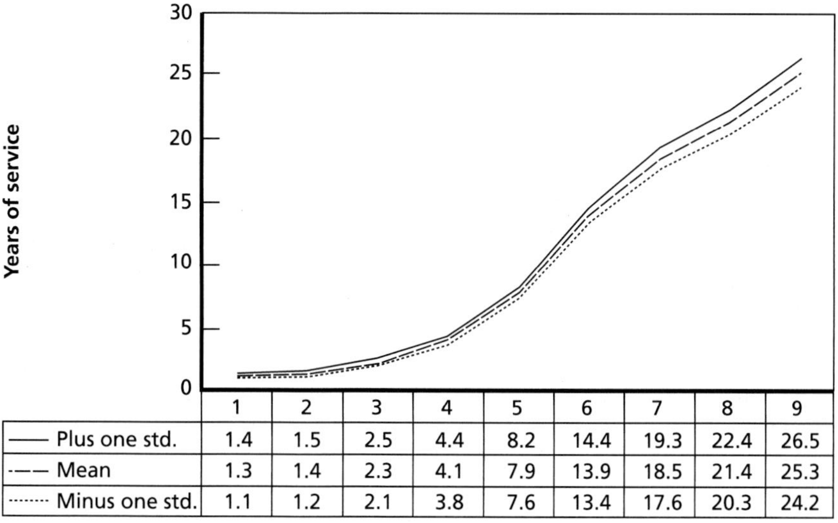

	1	2	3	4	5	6	7	8	9
—— Plus one std.	1.4	1.5	2.5	4.4	8.2	14.4	19.3	22.4	26.5
-—— Mean	1.3	1.4	2.3	4.1	7.9	13.9	18.5	21.4	25.3
······· Minus one std.	1.1	1.2	2.1	3.8	7.6	13.4	17.6	20.3	24.2

Enlisted grade

RAND *MG598-5.1*

Figure 5.2
YOS by Grade, Officer Corps

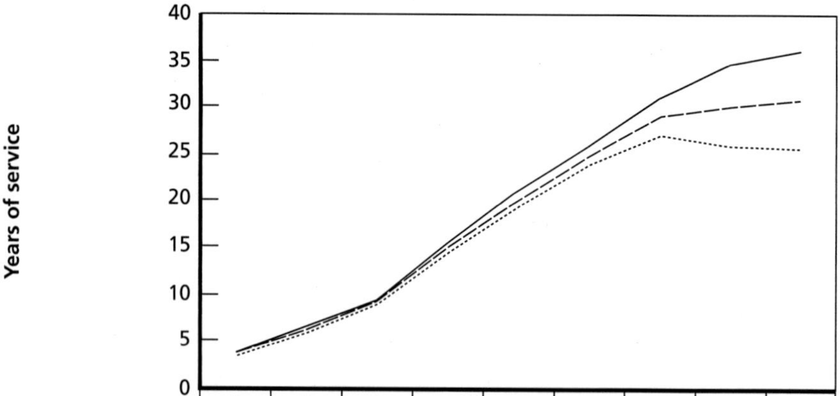

	1	2	3	4	5	6	7	8	9
—— Plus one std.	3.6	6.2	9.3	15.5	20.9	26.1	31.3	34.6	36.2
-— Mean	3.4	5.9	9.1	15.0	20.0	24.9	29.1	30.2	30.9
······· Minus one std.	3.3	5.7	8.8	14.4	19.2	23.8	26.9	25.9	25.6

Officer grade

RAND *MG598-5.2*

their personnel systems to the predictable decisions of the service members themselves. And, noted in Figures 3.2, 3.3, and 3.4, retention decisions on the part of military personnel are clearly driven by the pull of vesting in the very generous postretirement benefits that occur at YOS 20. Retention rates increase to very high levels in YOS 12–15 and then steadily creep up to over 90 percent over YOS 16–20. Then, in YOS 21, they plummet with the departure of over 40 percent of the enlisted force and 25 percent of the officer corps at that point. This is dramatic evidence of the role of the compensation system in shaping the force.

Figures 5.1, 5.2, and 5.3 illustrate some very basic facts about the promotion system. Figure 5.1 and Figure 5.2 show that there is very little variation in the pace of promotion, in both the enlisted force and the officer corps. These two figures show the average number of YOS for each grade and one standard deviation in either direction, above and below. There is very little variation in YOS for each grade; the standard deviation is only a few months. It is only at grade O-6 that

Figure 5.3
YOS by Grade, Coefficient of Variation

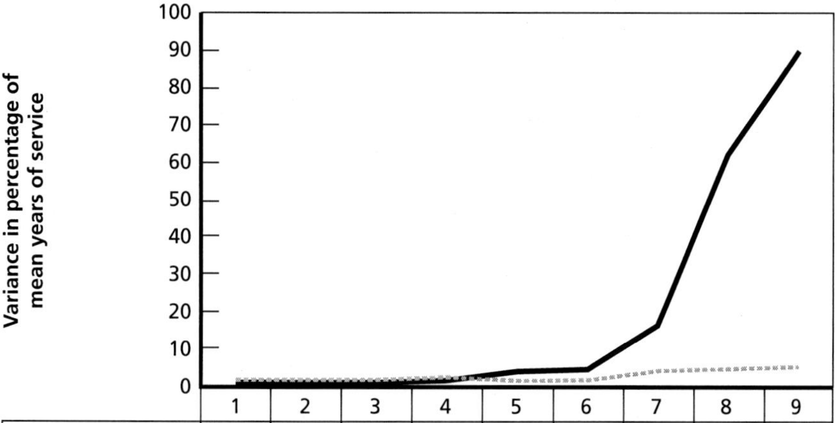

	1	2	3	4	5	6	7	8	9
Officer	0.6%	1.1%	0.8%	2.0%	3.9%	5.1%	16.6%	61.6%	90.0%
Enlisted	2.1%	1.6%	2.0%	2.2%	1.5%	2.0%	4.0%	5.1%	5.3%

Officer grade

RAND *MG598-5.3*

some difference in the promotion tempo for officers appears (a standard deviation of about one year); it then becomes quite wide at the general officer grades. In the enlisted force, the standard deviation is only about one year for each of the three highest grades.

Figure 5.3 reinforces these points, showing the ratio of the variance to the mean, which is known as the coefficient of variation. It is very low, only a few percentage points, except for the most senior grades. This indicates a promotion system driven by YOS. A service member who performs adequately can rest assured that he or she will be promoted simply by remaining in the service (at least to YOS 20), as long as the personnel system can find appropriate a job for him or her at the appropriate grade. In other words, the retention decision drives the promotion system, and the independent variable in this correlation is time, not grade. YOS determines grade, not the other way around.

All of this is not to suggest that the cliff-vesting system should be altered or eliminated—such a broad proposal would require a different study and investigation altogether. Rather, we only wish to stress the following conclusion: In a system of voluntary retention driven by the vesting rule, it becomes extraordinarily difficult to execute a policy of deliberate civilianization. Such a policy, if pursued on a large scale, requires important changes in the sizing of each cohort in the personnel inventory by using retention rates as deliberate management tools. For this reason alone, civilianization actions go against the deeply engrained practice of managing the force by adapting it to service members' voluntary retention decisions. Currently, the tools for managing retention are ineffective, other than the very limited up-or-out system, whereby someone passed over for promotion due to poor performance is finally forced to leave. In the absence of deliberate force-shaping tools and force-management principles, all civilianization policies immediately run into the following problem: If the services civilianize a large number of military positions, what are they to do with the personnel assigned to those positions in light of the fact that the current personnel system is structured to allow them to remain until they become eligible for the postretirement benefits that come with 20 YOS?

This is the central problem for any civilianization calculus. There may be strong financial reasons for pursuing civilianization and no functional imperatives that prevent the conversion of a military position to civilian; yet, the tools for effecting a civilianization policy may simply not exist at the present time. In a system where retirement benefits drive personnel systems, which in turn drive authorizations, it is simply not possible to formulate policies that apply at the authorization stage. Given the line of causation, it would be necessary to begin at the other end—with compensation and retirement vesting. In other words, compensation would need change to control retention, with civilianization pursued as a follow-on policy. One cannot lead from the rear; it must be done from the front.

This means that civilianization is, in reality, not a simple policy to effect—it is quite complex and cannot be pursued successfully without careful attention to the three inextricably entwined elements of any organization's human capital strategy: requirements, personnel management, and compensation. To successfully apply the calculus for estimating the cost of a military person-year developed in the preceding chapters, one must be mindful of the inseparable relationship between these aspects of human capital management. In an ideal world, the three elements would be balanced simultaneously. Yet past civilianization policies have always proceeded on the assumption that the personnel system can be quickly adapted to accommodate changing authorization levels. This does not seem to comport with reality.

Examples of Personnel Constraints Affecting Civilianization

The following example illustrates the difficulties encountered in seemingly simple civilianizations. Suppose some support function, e.g., maintenance functions on military equipment performed in one of the service's depots, is filled with NCOs in grades E-5 to E-7.[5] If these positions were offered up for civilianization, what savings might occur? One way estimate the gross savings by looking up the values for these grades in the data underlying Figure 4.4 above (i.e., the reduction in military pay and future benefits achieved by this civilianization decision). We could then make an estimate of the wages and salaries of the civilian personnel hired to replace the NCOs; Subtracting an estimate of the wages and benefits of the civilian personnel hired to replace the NCOs would indicate a very significant saving. However, does this simple procedure produce an accurate estimate?

We cannot answer that question without first investigating how the personnel system adapts to the civilianization. Typically, the affected military service would reassign the personnel who otherwise would have had their next tour at the depot. It is possible that this would upset planned career paths, because the formerly standard progression might have been a field assignment, followed by a depot assignment, then another field assignment, and after that perhaps a staff. The E-7s may have 16 or 17 YOS experience, so the service would do everything possible to find them another assignment so that they would not to lose

[5] Again, we note that an action such as this may affect career management. For example, if these positions are important feeders for later assignments, no savings may accrue as career tracks are adjusted. Since we do not know whether this is the case or not, we are using the probabilistic estimates developed here, i.e., using past average career tracks as stable.

vesting at YOS 20. Perhaps the E-5s have no more than 10 YOS experience and so may find their career prospects dimmed by the civilianization decision, causing some of them to decide to leave. Others may ask for retraining and stay in the service, but they may find promotion prospects dimmer. All of these are possible reactions by the personnelists and personnel in the affected service.

Where are the savings? Obviously, there are no savings at all if the persons formerly occupying the now civilianized positions are simply reassigned within their service. Meaningful savings occur only if the affected personnel were to leave the service entirely and choose to pursue civilian careers instead—perhaps even becoming employed by the very depot that civilianized their military positions. And if this were to happen, the savings for the FG would be reduced beyond buyout costs, as compared with the case where the persons who would have taken the positions as military instead leave and go to work for the private sector. The reason for this is that legislation passed in the 1990s allows former military personnel to buy into the federal retirement system and be given credit for their years of work in the military. Since the federal civilian retirement system is considerably less costly than the military, some savings would still occur, but not nearly as much as if the person took a job in a commercial enterprise. Hence, the net savings depend on the types of jobs taken by military personnel departing civilianized positions.

However, the gross and net savings also depend on how the military personnel system adapts to civilianizations. In their study of this issue, Gates and Robbert[6] make the important point that existing practices in the personnel system will spread out the effects of civilianizations across the entire force.

The triangles in Figure 5.4 illustrate a simplistic version of the services' personnel pyramids (i.e., the number of personnel distributed by grade), showing a broad base of entry-level personnel and a steep apex with a small number of persons in the most senior grades. The pyramids in the figure illustrate the enlisted force; the left pyramid indicates the civilianization of certain billets in the range of, say, E-3 to E-5.

---

6 Gates and Robbert, *Comparing the Costs of DoD Military and Civil Service Personnel.*

Figure 5.4
Possible Personnel System Adaptation to Civilianizations (1)

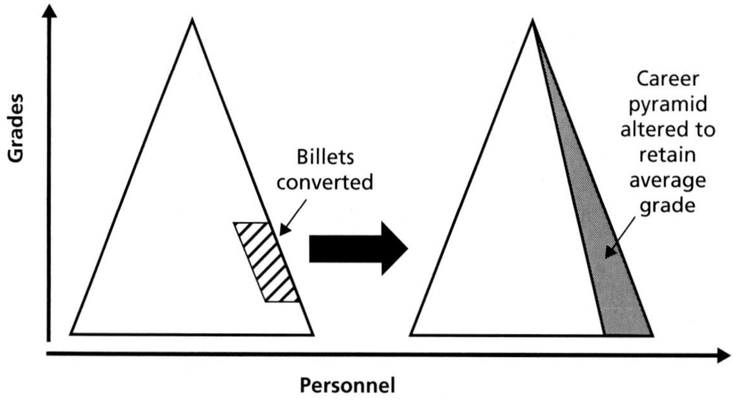

RAND *MG598-5.4*

Gates and Robbert are concerned with how this will affect promotions for the remaining personnel. In particular, the issue is how the flow of man-years will be affected, which depends on promotion speeds, compensation structure, and retention behaviors. We assume that a civilianization action occurs and that the affected personnel leave the service immediately; for example, they could be personnel who are at the end of their second reenlistment and who planned to leave anyway. Given that selection for promotion is based on a desire to maintain a stable distribution of personnel across grades, the implication is that promotions boards will speed up promotions from below to fill in the gap in the left pyramid from below and will slow down promotions in all grades above the gap, until the desired percentage distribution of grades across the force has been reestablished.[7] This is illustrated in the right-hand pyramid: The gap left in the force by the civilianization decision will smooth out, and the same conventional grade pyramid as existed beforehand will soon reemerge, albeit with a shorter base.

How quickly can this be accomplished? This depends on several factors. Note that the significant downsizings the services went through

---

7 Neither Gates and Robbert nor the present author contend that preservation of the existing grade pyramid represents an optimal policy.

in the first half of the 1990s created inventory imbalances that in some cases still affect various occupational specialties. The first of these factors is whether the civilianized personnel are given other assignments or are separated from the force. Under the idealistic assumption that they immediately leave the force, subsequent adjustments of the personnel system will be easy to accomplish. If, on the other hand, the affected personnel do not leave the service, other assignments will have to be found for them. The second factor is the number of personnel affected by the civilianization decision, and the third factor is the YOS and grades of the positions eliminated. The final factor is the guidance given to promotion boards regarding the percentage of each cohort eligible for civilianization that will be eligible for promotion.

If the personnel system adapts to civilianizations (as suggested by Gates and Robbert), then the per billet savings will be close to the weighted average of the change in grade distribution, comparing the initial state with a final state. That is, if the civilianized personnel were above the service's prior average grade, savings would be smaller than indicated by their grades in Figure 4.4 above; if they were below the average, they would obviously be somewhat greater. In section below, we will present computations that demonstrate how this process would work in practice.

Current events provide one more example of how important it is for the personnel system to adapt to civilianization actions by briefly relating a civilianization action currently in progress in the Army. Heavily engaged in deployments to Afghanistan and Iraq, the Army needs to increase authorizations in the units assigned to these missions to sustain reasonable tour lengths for affected personnel. With a given ceiling to total authorizations, the Army did not have the option of hiring new personnel; rather, it was told by OSD to find the required funds by civilianizing some military positions and to transfer the military authorizations freed up by those civilianizations to the units with the greatest needs at the present time. The Army proposes to do this by transferring authorizations and assigned personnel from the institutional Army (known as the TDA Army, for Table of Distributions and Allowances) to the field Army (known as the TO&E Army, for Table of Organization and Equipment).

There are two problems with this process. In Figure 5.5, the vertical axis represents officer grades and the corresponding average YOS for each grade. The vertical bars on the left illustrate the TO&E Army; the two versions of the TDA Army are illustrated by the bars on the right. One bar represents temporary assignments to the institutional Army, such as may occur regularly in a standard military career primarily focused on field activities. The other bar represents various career fields that imply a permanent assignment to the TDA Army. The arrows illustrate fairly typical career paths that often occur in the Army. A junior officer begins serving in field units, then serves a tour in an institutional assignment, and then gets promoted, whereupon he or she is reassigned to the field again. This cycle may be repeated two or three times. Some personnel move out of field units permanently and stay in the TDA Army.

The implication of this personnel practice is that the average grade in the TDA Army is one full grade higher than in the TO&E Army; this holds for both officers and enlisted personnel. Furthermore, personnel typically assigned to TO&E units have less experience for every

Figure 5.5
Possible Personnel System Adaptation to Civilianizations (2)

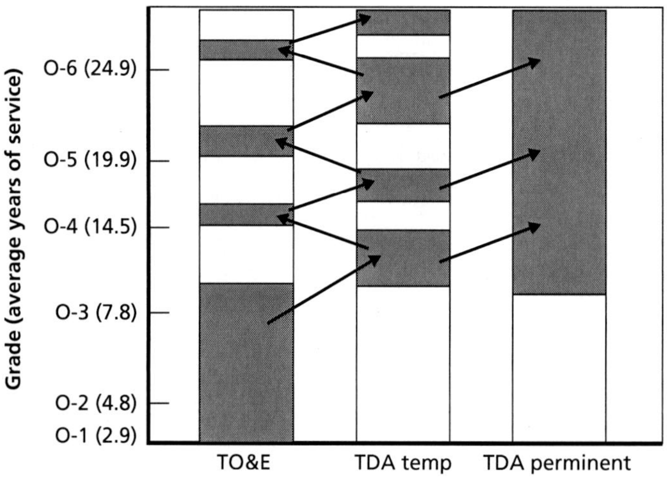

RAND *MG598-5.5*

given grade. The problem is this: When the Army wants to reassign a significant number of authorized positions from the institutional Army to field units, it faces a grade and experience imbalance. Again, if the numbers are not significant, the personnel system may be able to identify the right personnel in the TDA Army who will neatly fit into the TO&E Army, but, if the size of transfers is very large, there will be a mismatch that may require a few promotion cycles to work through.

Since this was not a civilianization action pursued for the purposes of creating savings, as in the case of the Navy and the Air Force, the second problem the Army faced is that it was not allowed to receive the additional operations and maintenance funding required to pay for newly created civilian billets.[8] It had to identify some bill payers within the Army's budget from which to transfer the funding to pay for the civilianization action in those units and commands where the new positions were created. This was in spite of a general agreement that the Army needed to beef up the TO&E units in question, and that civilianization certainly would cost significantly less than increasing military authorizations. This is a case where the calculus in the preceding chapters would be applicable. Applying the Gates and Robbert argument, the average grade of the military personnel pyramid would be unaffected by the transfer of personnel from TDA to TO&E—although it might have raised the TO&E experience level somewhat, it probably increased the grade levels and average YOS in the personnel assigned to TDA activities. Hence, for cost comparison purposes, the average costs from the data underlying Figure 4.4 indicate the gross savings, from which the costs for the newly hired civilian personnel are deducted to estimate the net savings. No doubt they would have been substantial.

---

[8] In effect, the Army had to increase its total personnel inventory, military and civilian, within a given total budget.

The Spoils and Their Division

This section will demonstrate how the calculus developed in this study can be applied in practice, in consideration of the relationship to the personnel system just discussed. This discussion will indicate by how much the SMCRs underestimate the real economic benefits from a civilianization action. This section will also show how these savings can actually be recovered by DoD in the budget process through a method that does not require legislation. In other words, it is possible, without changing anything in the actuarial methods, to allow a military service full credit for all savings to the FG deriving from a civilianization decision. This has important implications for future force management.

The steady-state inventory projections developed by the DoD Office of the Actuary can be used to demonstrate how the calculus should be applied in practice. Unlike actual inventories presently available on real service data, the actuaries' steady-state data are free of the peaks and valleys that show today's remnants of past personnel actions that are such prominent features of the real data. The actuaries' steady-state inventories have already been illustrated in Figure 3.6 above.

Note that this is obviously a very contrived example. No drawdown in DoD has ever been attempted across the board, as the following the computations assume. In reality, each military service would perform a drawdown suited to its operational requirements and current inventory, as shaped by past personnel and manpower decisions. Various special rules, such as a strong desire to protect as many people close to retirement vesting as possible, may also play into how the drawdown is shaped in practice. Furthermore, particular functional communities may be directly targeted for more aggressive culling than others. This means that, to compute the actually realized savings, the methodology developed here requires detailed data on retention (continuation) and retirement rates by YOS and grade that may be very specific, down to the level of certain career fields. Thus, while our methodology has the advantage of allowing more precise estimates of savings to the FG from eliminating certain military positions, it comes at the cost of requiring more detailed data and analysis than the simple application of the SMCRs requires.

In our example, we assume that DoD takes a reduction of the personnel inventory by 5 percent, both officers and enlisted personnel, and that the entire drawdown is concentrated in four year-groups, YOS 10–13. This is obviously an extreme and even unrealistic example, but it is exactly the kind of action illustrated in Figure 5.4 above.[9] First, we trace the effects of this action on the inventory; second, we compute the total personnel cost savings according to two different methods.

To see the effects of the drawdown, the inventory has to be aged, one year at a time. That is, we must make some assumptions about retention rates by YOS. To simplify the analysis, we assume that the transition probabilities from one year to the next remain completely unchanged—which, for reasons that will immediately become very obvious below, is not how a service would act in reality. However, since there are many ways of managing the retention rates through promotion boards and buyouts, to name but two tools available, there is no one "best" solution to how to manage the inventory—never mind that there simply is no universal solution to military personnel inventory management problems. So, given a 5 percent total reduction in force spread out over YOS 10–13 and a constant vector of retention rates by YOS, how many years will it take for the force to absorb the "bathtub" and return to a steady-state shape where every cohort is reduced by 5 percent? This, as illustrated by Figure 5.4, is what one would expect when applying standard force management principles. Figures 5.6 and 5.7 below show the results of this analysis for officers and enlisted personnel.

In both figures, the initial effects of the drawdown is illustrated by "hanging baskets" underneath the steady-state baseline in the graph. For each year, these baskets will wander one step to the right, as the inventory is aged through time (the figures show these baskets for a few select years only). Finally, the figures show that, after the inventory has adjusted fully, a new steady-state is achieved where all year-groups have been reduced uniformly by 5 percent.

---

[9] In reality, drawdowns are not managed by YOS, but by grade and occupational specialties. All the arguments and numbers presented below could easily be translated to grades, so nothing substantive is affected by our choice of expositional techniques.

Figure 5.6
Inventory Drawdown and Adjustments, Officers

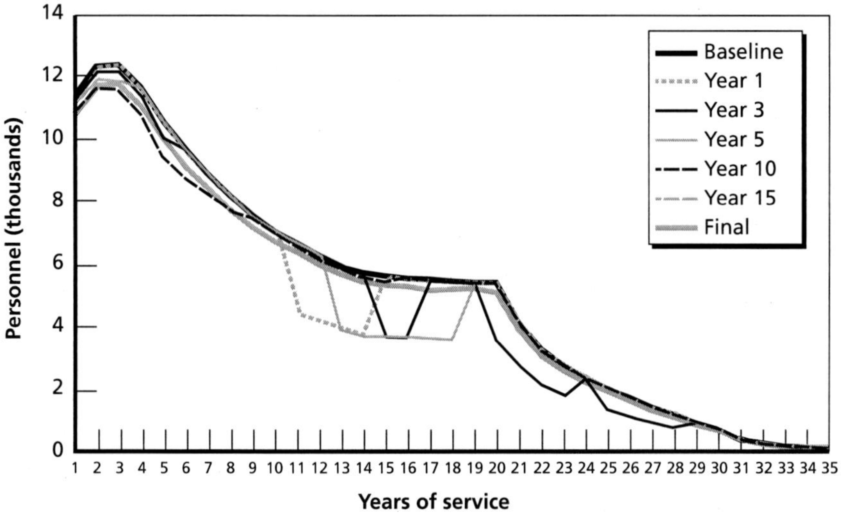

RAND *MG598-5.6*

Figure 5.7
Inventory Drawdown and Adjustments, Enlisted Personnel

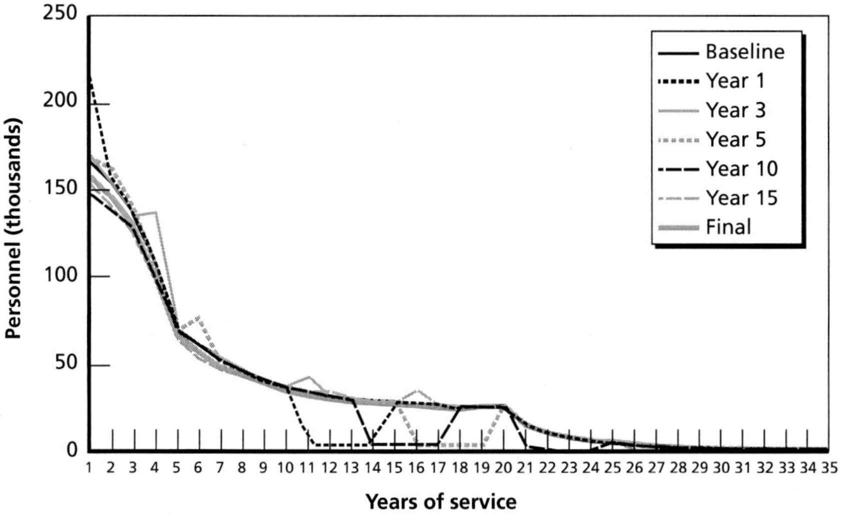

RAND *MG598-5.7*

Two issues of interest arise. The first is the answer to the question: How many years does it take for the inventory to return completely to its original shape, i.e., a situation where each cohort has exactly the same percentage of the total as before the drawdown? One might guess that this would take the length of a full career, say 35 years. The actual answer is 100 years, and the reason can be seen most clearly in Figure 5.7.

This leads to the second point: To reduce the overall inventory by 5 percent, it is necessary to increase the initial inventory (here, for simplicity, we have increased the entry cohort, as can be seen in the dotted line for the first year on the enlisted figure). For this inventory, the steady-state entry cohort is 166,000. It turns out that if the entry cohort is kept at 166,000 immediately upon the drawdown, this leads to a total reduction of the force by 8.9 percent, or almost twice the size of the intended drawdown of 5 percent. It seems completely counter-intuitive that, in order to effect a 5 percent drawdown of the force by reductions of older year-groups, it becomes necessary to increase the entry cohort. The reason lies in the effects of aging the force from one year to the next. The following computation calculates the number of enlisted personnel taken out from the baseline: $0.05 \times 1{,}200{,}000 = 60{,}000$. However, when this is applied to the inventory, the inventory has aged by one year and all year-groups have experienced normal attrition. Thus, the 60,000 reduction turns out to be a full 8.9 percent of the next year's inventory, which must then be compensated by an increase in the initial cohort to make the net drawdown equal the planned 5 percent.[10] The initial cohort has to increase by a full 28 percent over its steady-state value, from 166,000 to 213,000 (see the dotted line to the very left in Figure 5.7). This huge bump in the first year then ages through the inventory, which can be seen by the little peaks in Figure 5.7, and then sets up secondary ripple effects on entry cohorts at later times.

The net result of this analysis is the startling fact that it takes a full 100 years for the inventory to settle back to its original shape. In reality,

---

[10] The Navy has encountered exactly such an effect in its current drawdown and has decided to spread the increase in the entry cohort over two years.

after about 35 years, or a full career for one cohort, it is approximately back to normal, but the full effects will not peter out for three complete generations. Obviously, the time it takes for the inventory to adjust can be shortened considerably by managing the transition probabilities for each year-group. As noted, this can be done through a combination of new guidelines to promotion panels (promote a lower percentage of fat year-groups and higher percentage of lean year-groups) and affirmative steps such as buyouts or early retirements. The exact time it takes for the inventory to settle down after a drawdown clearly depends on the size of the reduction taken, the year-groups affected, and the precise affirmative management steps taken to smooth out the inventory as quickly as possible. This is what makes inventory adjustments an art form: They rely on fairly simple arithmetic but require careful management decisions about how to distribute the drawdown actions across occupations, year-groups, and grades in a manner that best supports the future force. In principle, the quickest way to get the grade pyramid to settle down would obviously be to take a given percentage out of each year-group; however, this may violate the perceived commitment made to personnel in the career force that they will be allowed to stay to YOS 20 and retire with full benefits. Note that all of these decisions will affect the savings achievable from career terminations and civilianizations. A complete calculus would compare the cost of the initial force with the cost of a newly established equilibrium force and discount all the cost differentials between them back to the time of the decision. Such a calculus goes considerably beyond what is attempted here but would be conceptually more correct.

Given the limitations highlighted above, the savings from the drawdown just described can now be computed. We will compare two methods: that mandated in the DoD Comptroller's official mandated procedure, and the method developed in this study. The preceding computations show the personnel inventory by YOS and by grade. The data in Table 3.1 can be used for the official SMCRs with which the annual savings over the six-year budget period (called the FYDP, for Future Years Defense Program) can be computed. For the values resulting from our method, we look to Table 4.7. Figures 5.8 and 5.9 show the results of these computations.[11]

Both figures show the discounted present value of postretirement benefits that will not be paid to the four cohorts affected by the drawdown, adjusted for the probability that the personnel affected would reach retirement eligibility at 20 YOS (and also for those who would have been likely to stay beyond, as discussed in the preceding section). In the first year of the FYDP, this then shows a very large savings for the drawdown: $8 billion for officers and $77 billion for enlisted personnel. For the remaining years, the savings include only RMC but not accrual, since the personnel separated in the drawdown have already, in effect, since arithmetically assigned their retirement benefits by the savings taken in the first year, so no accrual payment would be required. For this reason, the SMCRs yield a much lower return to civilianizations in the first year, but somewhat more (by the 31.5 percent accrual factor used) in the ensuing years.

The difference between the two methods is significant. The economic method computes the net savings to the FG over the budget period, but the SMCRs only provide the outlays in the DoD budget. As a result, the SMCRs give DoD credit only for no more than 54 percent of total savings for officers and 41 percent of the savings for enlisted personnel. This would greatly affect the size of any drawdown undertaken to create budget savings. Suppose, for example, that DoD wishes to pay for increased outlays for modernization by transferring funding, within a given total defense budget, from the personnel account to the acquisition account. If, say, a transfer of $100 billion is required over the FYDP, then using the SMCRs would lead to a drawdown of some X% of the personnel inventory, however it would be spread out. Depending on the year-groups and the mix of officers and enlisted personnel affected, the percentage X may vary significantly for the same total savings. Using our method, however, the drawdown would only have to be some fraction b of that X, where the factor b would be less than

---

[11] Recall that the figures in Table 4.7 represent gross (not net) saving estimates. Actual (achievable) saving will be less, perhaps considerably less, than shown in Figure 5.8 for officers and in Figure 5.9 for enlisted personnel.

Figure 5.8
Savings from Civilianizations, Two Methods, Officers

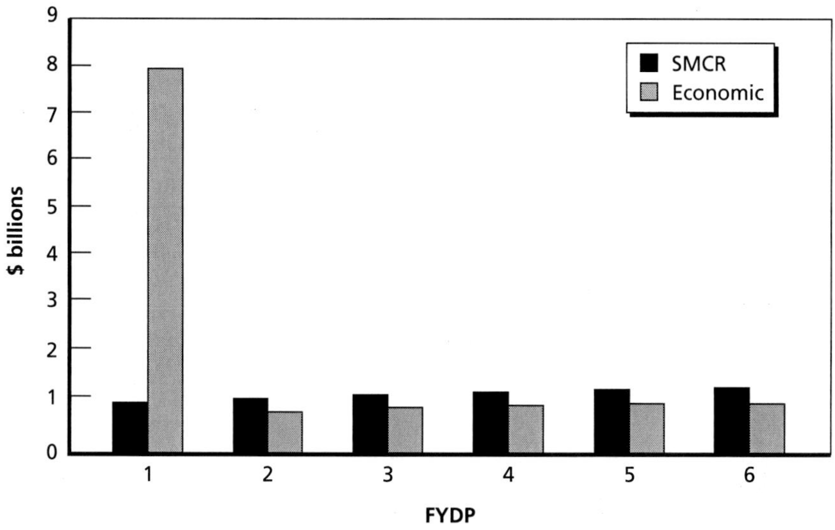

RAND *MG598-5.8*

Figure 5.9
Savings from Civilianizations, Two Methods, Enlisted Personnel

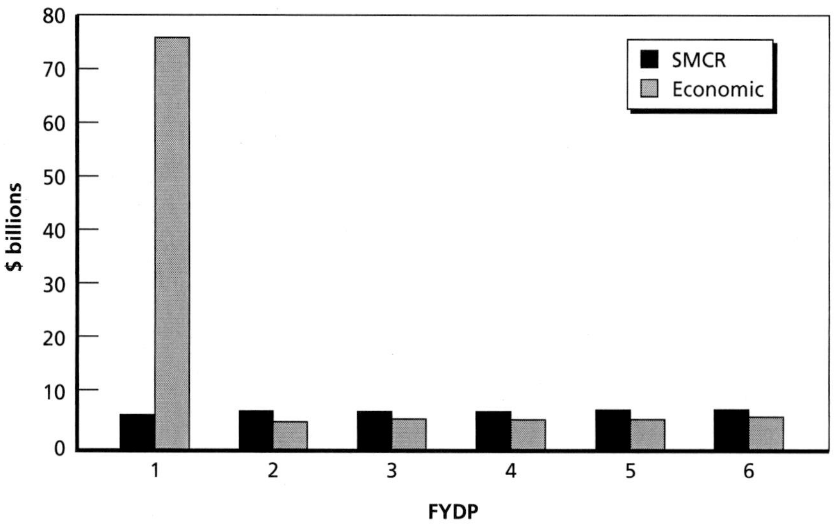

RAND *MG598-5.9*

one, and again depend critically on the year-groups and officer/enlisted mix affected. In this extreme computational example, where a uniform 5 percent drawdown was done by a reduction of four year-groups, the SMCRs provide only a weighted average of 43 percent of the total savings to the FG. In other words, in this example, if the total savings estimated using the SMCR is the desired goal, the total drawdown would be almost 2.5 times as large as would really be required under our more economically correct accounting method. Using the SMCRs would cause a much greater turbulence for the personnel system and individual careers than would our method. Use of the SMCRs appears both inefficient and deeply unfair to the personnel affected.

An obvious question is whether it would be possible, under present legislation and budget accounting rules, to realize these savings for DoD. That is, can one design a legally defensible accounting method by which DoD could capture the total savings to the FG, thus providing the military services with the proper payback for the wrenching decisions that are required in every drawdown? As it turns out, the Air Force and the Navy have both recently attempted this, and have both been turned back.

In the case of the Air Force, which is currently planning on a drawdown of some 40,000 personnel in order to fund the acquisition of future aircraft, the question was put to the DoD Comptroller and to OMB whether the savings in reduced future outlays for postretirement benefits could be used to pay for increased buyouts for separated personnel, which obviously would have reduced the net expected savings from the force reductions. Author interviews with Air Force officials revealed that the answer the Air Force received was that, as long as the Congressional Budget Office (CBO) would allow this under its budget scoring rules, the Air Force could go ahead. However, CBO denied the proposal, using the standard argument that additional current outlays (the increased buyouts for personnel) cannot be offset against reductions in future outlays, especially since in this case the reductions in future outlays would occur only in a quite distant future.

In the case of the Navy, which is also planning to fund acquisitions through personnel drawdowns, the question was raised as to whether it would be allowable to count savings occurring later in the

FYDP programming period as offsets against increased outlays in the beginning of the FYDP. Again, this was turned back under CBO budget scoring rules for exactly the same reasons. For now, discussion is closed on these issues within DoD. The services are only allowed to count the savings to DoD, per the SMCRs, and not the full amount of the savings to the entire FG, even though the former can be accomplished in a manner quite consistent with federal budget rules.

The problem the Air Force and the Navy both encountered was the CBO scoring rule that prohibits offsets of current outlays against future savings—a seemingly sensible rule intended to prohibit the most egregious budget shenanigans. However, if there were a way to offset the increased outlays against reductions in contemporaneous outlays, there would be no problem. As it turns out, there is such a mechanism available through the accrual system, as follows.

In the above example of drawing down the four year-groups in YOS 10–13, it is obvious that the accrual system has already worked as designed to set aside contributions in the trust funds for the future benefits of the members in these cohorts. That is, the present value of the future benefits saved at the point the personnel in these cohorts separate from the force has already been paid for. Hence, their separation provides an unanticipated actuarial gain to the trust fund. The issue we are facing is that this gain accrues to the FG, not to the employing agency, i.e., DoD. Chapter Six presents a discussion of the controversy over this method and shows that, while it is standard in the FG, it is actually a procedure that is prohibited for use in private defined benefit pension plans. The question addressed here is: Is it possible, within current budget rules and accrual practices, to allocate the actuarial gain to DoD rather than to the trust fund?

The obvious suggestion would that, if DoD has already paid in accrual contributions on behalf of the separating members of the force, then the unanticipated actuarial gain created by the drawdown can be recovered through reduced accrual for a suitable period of time. Since the trust fund has realized a gain as a result of an action taken at the discretion of Congress and DoD to reduce the total force size, the reduced contributions will not affect its future ability to pay all required benefits to vested retirees. Thus, offsetting the increased current outlays for weapons acquisitions or for personnel buyouts more generous than provided for under current legislation against a reduction in current accrual payments offers the easiest and most direct way to capture the actuarial gains in the present budget. This method clearly is consistent with the CBO requirements, since both increased outlays and savings are accounted for in the same budget year.

One significant hurdle would seem to make this simple solution impossible to effect: Title 10 contains specific provisions that the required accrual amount each year shall be computed by a board of actuaries and put into the President's budget. This is done in order to ensure that DoD pays in the actuarially fair amount each year and does not give in to any temptation to underfund the retirement and health trust funds. Since the particular formula used by the actuaries requires only forward-looking calculations, it does not allow DoD to reduce accrual payments in order to capture past actuarial gains.[12] Therefore, many have concluded that the obvious and simple way for DoD to capture the total savings from drawdowns is closed by legislation.

This is simply not true, due to a basic and fundamental constitutional fact. According to the statute, DoD is required to put into the President's budget an amount calculated by the boards of actuaries. This provision is clearly unconstitutional on two separate grounds. First, the boards are not made up of federal employees. Both the Retirement Board of Actuaries and the Health Board of Actuaries are constituted as federal advisory boards that do not report to any appointed federal official, the members of which have no legal standing as federal officials. Thus, their opinions can, at best, have the standing as advisory, in spite of any statutory requirements. No statute can demand that a federal official obey the advice of a nonfederal member of an outside board. Second, the President's budget proposal is just that—a proposal to Congress of the amount the administration believes it will take to fund all federal programs over the budget horizon. The proposal belongs exclusively to the President, and he may suggest any changes he

---

[12] In fact, the DoD method as implemented in the SMCRs completely ignores the fact that the trust funds represent an asset to the FG. We return to this issue in greater detail in Chapter Six.

considers appropriate. Congress then has the constitutional obligation to consider the proposals and to enact into legislation those it regards as having the most merit. This system and it effectively prohibits Congress from mandating what the President must include in his budget proposal. The President is free to include anything he considers important; it is then up to Congress to act, or not, on those proposals.

Therefore, there are no legislative roadblocks to using a more precise method to determine the correct amount of credit for drawdown decisions. Our method for doing so is as follows.

In the budget, there would be three lines for total accrual contributions in any one year. The first line would be calculated as currently done; i.e., it would show the accrual amount for the funding of future benefits as proposed by the Boards of Actuaries. The second line would be the offset, computed as demonstrated in this section; i.e., it would show the amount of reduction in current accruals that can be gained by the proposed drawdown. The third line would show the difference between the first and the second lines, indicating the net accrual contribution that the President proposes Congress appropriate in the legislated budget. This makes the procedure completely transparent and comports with CBO scoring rules. It would then be up to Congress to determine whether it will accept the proposed reduction in accrual. Should Congress determine that it will not accept the proposal, the implication is that it then must either reduce the desired increased outlays on acquisitions or buyouts or increase the size of the drawdown. This is completely within the prerogative of Congress to determine.

Now the following question arises: Using this procedure, how much of the annually required accrual, as determined by the Boards of Actuaries, could the DoD offset using the estimates from the example above? The answer can be arrived at by taking the total savings over the FYDP, shown above, and smoothing them out evenly over the FYDP to avoid the very extreme peak in the first year that otherwise would occur. That is, we suggest that the President's budget include a level annual amount, adjusted only for the annual inflation rate. The results are shown in Figure 5.10 in comparison with the total amount of accrual that DoD would be charged with.

In this particular case, since the savings from a fairly large drawdown have been spread over six years, it happens that the total amounts saved, in every year, are greater than the annually required accrual payments by more than one-third. In principle, that would mean that DoD could claim a direct payment back from the trust funds, amounting to negative accrual for these years. However, there is no provision in law that would allow that. Therefore, the only remedy for DoD would be to limit the drawdown by computing exactly the right percentage of personnel drawdown, by year-group and officer/enlisted, so that it would lead to savings exactly equal to the accrual amount. This is a straightforward computation, and we do not need to pursue it further here.

Figure 5.10
Annualized Total Accrual Savings per Two Methods

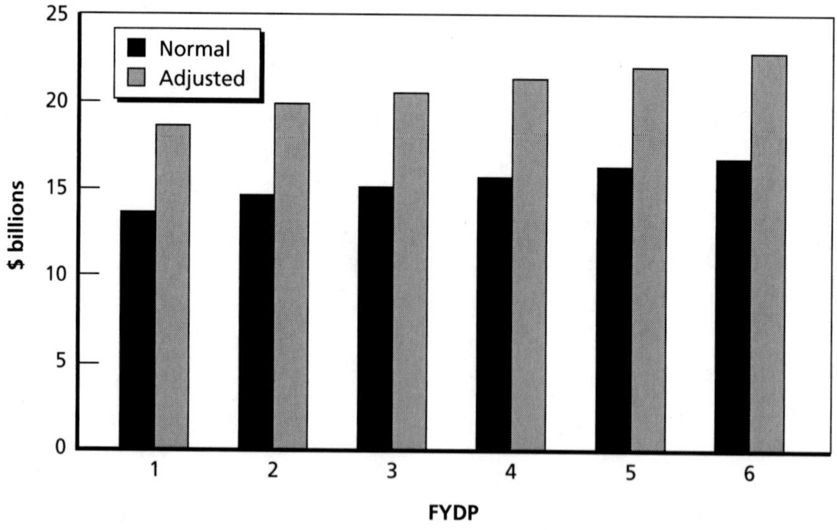

RAND *MG598-5.10*

The Practice of Drawdowns

An actual application of this method using current data should dispel any notion that the preceding is just an academic exercise. As has been noted, the Air Force is at the present time pursuing a drawdown of its personnel inventory by around 40,000. Using data from December 2006, we will illustrate how this drawdown is executed and briefly suggest the relevance of the preceding analysis to the decisions the Air Force has to make. Figures 5.11 and 5.12 show the present inventory and the planned adjustments for fiscal year 2007, i.e., for only one of the years of the planned drawdown.[13]

The graph of the officer corps shows each year-group for the last 30 years, back to those who entered in 1977, represented by vertical bars. The solid line indicates the desired inventory in FY 2009, and the diagonal sections on top of some (most) year-groups indicate the current actions taken to cull the inventory and shape it to the desired FY 2009 sustainment pattern. The chart also indicates the particular personnel actions that the Air Force intends to undertake to shape the inventory. From left to right in the figure, these are force shaping board (FSB), reduction-in-force (RIF), voluntary separation program (VSP), and selective early retirement board (SERB). FSB is a process by which certain specialties (occupations) are reduced; in this particular case, FSB was applied to two very recent year-groups. The members who were selected have to leave the Air Force and receive no compensation for the loss of what perhaps quite a few of them were hoping to make a full career. Members of YOS 6–18 who are let go involuntarily receive payments under VSP. VSP allows compensation for 10 percent of the highest salary multiplied by the number of months served. (VSP authority provided in FY 2006 allowed two times this formula; it was expanded to four times by the FY 2007 National Defense Authorization Act.)[14] Finally, for certain occupations and year-groups among

[13] Both graphs were produced in the office of the Deputy Chief of Staff of the Air Force for Personnel, and hence represent official Air Force data.

[14] We cannot know (except for probabilistic averages based on past retention patterns) who in this group would have left before vesting and who would never have vested. Therefore, some individuals lose the difference between the buyout value and whatever retirement they

Figure 5.11
Air Force Force-Shaping Actions 2007, Officers

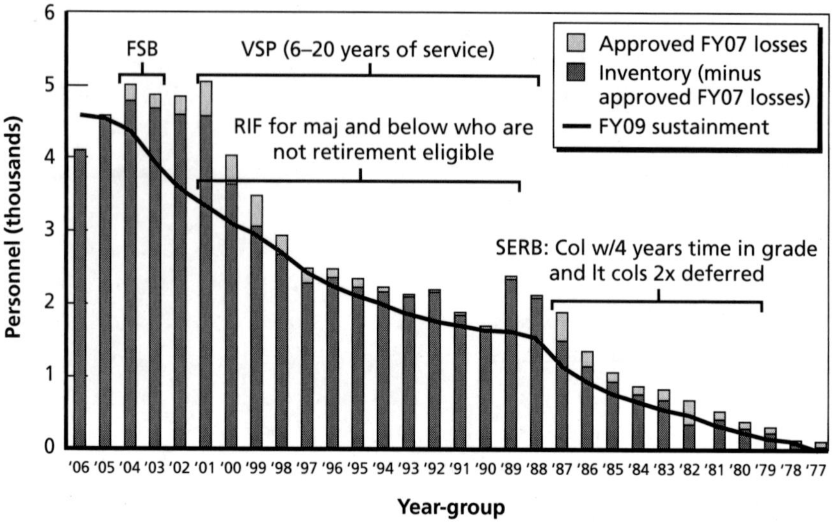

RAND *MG598-5.11*

Figure 5.12
Air Force Force-Shaping Actions 2007, Enlisted Personnel

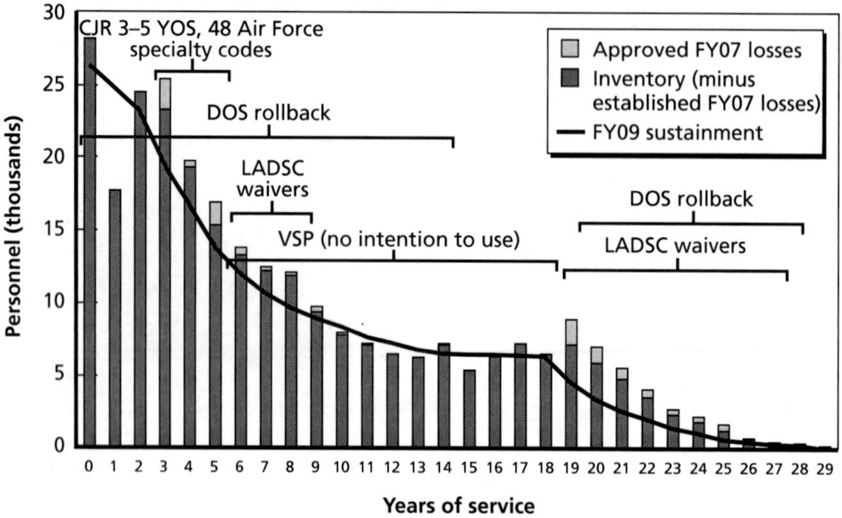

RAND *MG598-5.12*

those above 20 YOS (i.e., those who have already vested in postretirement benefits), a number of people were "SERBed," meaning that they were simply asked to retire before they expected or were planning to. All of these actions lead to reductions in the personnel inventory. The actual savings naturally depend on the specific earnings (i.e., grade and time-in-grade, combined with YOS). The cost of reducing the force depends on the number of takers of the separation compensation paid to some of them. Next, we look at how the enlisted force was shaped in these efforts.

For YOS 4–6, the Air Force terminated some people but provided two possible transition opportunities for them. If eligible, and if positions were available, they were offered career job reservations (CJRs), meaning that affected individuals could apply for retraining into other occupations in the Air Force—an option not offered to officers. In addition (and not shown in the chart), there is a program called blue-to-green, which encourages separated personnel, both enlisted and officer, to apply for positions in the Army. This is naturally a difficult and risky transition. Separated Air Force personnel choosing to go into the Army will receive credit for years served and may be allowed to continue in the same grade. However, the transfer will undoubtedly require retraining into new occupations, and it is not known at this point how competitive these individuals will be for future promotions. At this point, the total number of blue-to-green acceptances is in the hundreds, so only a few people have availed themselves this opportunity.

The other two tools used to shape the enlisted force are date-of-separation (DOS) rollback and limited active-duty service commitment (LADSC). Both of these tools are used to force out a member at a point earlier than when he or she was planning to leave. In occupations and year-groups targeted for such culling, the Air Force may know when someone is going to leave, either because a person's enlistment period is ending or because a service commitment required (e.g., as payback for an educational benefit paid by the Air Force), and in these cases DOS rollback and LADSC may be applied to save the last

---

would have earned had they been allowed to stay; others, however, receive compensation for retirement benefits that they would never have received.

year or so of a member's enlistment period. The figure also shows that, although the VSP option is available for enlisted personnel as well as for officers, the Air Force does not plan to use it at the present time. That is, no compensation for loss of future benefits will be paid to enlisted personnel other than what they may have qualified for by serving the full 20 YOS.

How much will the Air Force save by separating these people? The answer can be determined by looking at the SMCRs. In some cases, the savings are small, since only the last year of service is eliminated; in other cases, entire career fields are reduced to small numbers, and no new entry is allowed. But even in these cases, savings are limited to those provided by the SMCRs. The fact that a full 40,000 positions will be eliminated only over a few years and the concomitant significant savings in outlays for future benefits realized from this action will not benefit the Air Force under the DoD actuaries' method. A quick computation of the net savings could be computed by applying the Gates-Robbert argument and computing the average compensation of the members of the FY 2009 desired inventory (the solid line in the diagrams) and multiplying that number by the number of personnel saved, plus the PV of all future postretirement benefits for the average member of that inventory (i.e., applying the values in Table 4.7 above). Since these savings would be significantly higher than allowed by the SMCRs, the number of personnel affected could be proportionately reduced, or more generous buyout options provided to involuntarily separated members. From this perspective, the SMCRs are not just analytically misguided, they are also fundamentally inefficient and unfair to the personnel whose livelihood is affected by their application to estimating the cost of a military person-year.

Concluding Comment

The lack of credit the Army received for its civilianization actions and the limited reimbursement provided to the Navy and the Air Force for theirs point to an endemic weakness in the current policies effected to encourage civilianization. DoD senior management has not provided strong enough budgetary incentives for the military services to pursue aggressive civilianizations. Even when the services follow DoD guidance, as in the case of the Air Force and the Navy, the amount of savings for which they get credit is limited by the DoD Comptroller's SMCRs. Since the calculus in the preceding chapter has demonstrated that the real economic cost of military personnel is significantly higher than the SMCRs, it is obvious that the services are not being allowed to capitalize on the real savings from civilianizations.[15]

The reason for this is that our computations are based on total FG costs, not just on DoD budget outlays. Currently, DoD pays only the accrual charge for postretirement benefits, which, as we have demonstrated, is only a fraction of the total cost of these benefits to the total federal budget. In addition, our method includes the costs of the TFL program. However, beginning in the FY 2007 budget, the Department of the Treasury, not DoD, will be responsible for paying the required accrual for military personnel into the TFL Trust Fund.[16]

The vast majority of the savings in a civilianization action comes, in our calculations, from the reduction of future outlays required to fund benefits for retired personnel. Under current budget rules, this means that the cost avoidance achieved by civilianization in DoD is limited to the accrual amount, and not even the accrual amount for all postretirement benefits at that.[17]

---

[15] We have noted above how the law allows military personnel who leave before vesting to enter civil service and get constructive credit for their years in the military. If we knew these transition probabilities, as well as the further probabilities of this particular group staying in federal service by year, we could deduct the present value of these future outlays in computing the net savings from civilianizations. We leave this refinement aside, and note only that a more precise calculus would take it into consideration.

[16] Congress did this in 2004 in order to reduce the appropriations required by DoD during the global war on terrorism. See Public Law 108-375, *The Ronald W. Reagan National Defense Authorization Act for 2005*, Section 725.

[17] Through a unique action (which has not become a precedent), something akin to this was actually accomplished during the military drawdown in the early 1990s. When DoD drew down its personnel, the argument was made that much of the past accrual already made for those who were going to leave the military should be repaid to DoD. Congress agreed to split the gains from this: DoD was allowed to allot some of these savings to increased acquisition; the rest was essentially spent by Congress.

Two central points have arisen from our analysis. Large-scale civilianizations inevitably require that the three legs of the human capital strategy can work together: requirements determination, personnel system adjustments, and the compensation system that supports them both. In an institutional setting where retention is driven by cliff vesting, it is difficult to see how senior DoD managers can ever induce significant conversions of personnel in the career force (i.e., among exactly those personnel likely to cost the FG the most in retirement benefits). Looked at this way, it would seem very desirable to use civilianization as a tool for significant force shaping. It is not unlikely that there are many positions occupied by personnel in the YOS 15–20 that could be civilianized at considerable savings to the FG. Obviously, this would require some method for buyouts, such as those that were successfully implemented during the drawdown of the early 1990s. Since the savings from reducing future outlays for retired personnel are potentially huge, it would seem that the funding for such buyouts could be made available. Furthermore, given that we know from past drawdowns that the personal discount rates of military personnel are 18 percent or higher,[18] it is obvious that huge savings are possible by eliminating military positions and offering equitable buyouts to the affected personnel.

However, this conclusion must be weighed against the important limitations imposed by the current budget process. A private corporation that reduces future outlays will see an immediate increase in its net worth and can find various ways of turning that into ready investment funding. This is simply not possible for DoD under current budget rules. Hence, even though the methods developed in this study indicate a potential for very significant savings from aggressive civilianizations, only a concerted engagement by Congress could possibly establish procedures for allowing those savings to be funneled back to current decisionmakers. That is, although we have constructed a correct calculus, significant changes in policy and practice are required before its practical application can be realized. As long as DoD can only recover cost savings from reductions in current outlays, the lim-

---

[18] This number is estimated by Warner and Pleeter, "The Personnel Discount Rate." It reflects the experience of the large drawdown in the 1990s.

ited, even faulty, accounting based on reductions in accrual outlays would seem the only practical way to estimate savings from civilianizations. Never mind that the potential savings from civilianization seem huge; for DoD, most of these savings are likely to remain unrealized until the powerful incentives described in this chapter are fully incorporated into the budget process.

The method presented and applied in this chapter provides better estimates of the total savings to the FG from DoD civilianizations than the use of the current SMCRs. Hence, every civilianization or force shaping action that is driven by a desire for particular budget savings (e.g., to finance modernization activities) causes more separations of military personnel than required. It can hardly be said that this is a fair system that does not provide the proper credit to the military services that pursue aggressive force management, since the results are terminations of personnel who are eminently qualified to stay. This is particularly the case if, as we have argued, there is a method that can be pursued by which Congress would grant these savings to DoD.

CHAPTER SIX

Final Issues, Conclusions, and Recommendations

Military Versus Civilian: A Hypothetical Cost Comparison

In a hypothetical computation to study the cost implications of civilianizing the 20-year career of a typical newly commissioned officer or an entry-level enlisted person, what salaries could the FG pay the civilians while maintaining the same life-cycle personnel costs? This computation can be made fairly easily using the same assumptions employed by the DoD actuaries.

The life-cycle cost to the FG of a new member of the military who will stay 20 years can be computed the following way:

- Basic pay and allowances for the average grade by YOS are inflated by an assumed pay growth of 3.75 percent per year for the appropriate number of years, until YOS 20.
- Future TFL claims are computed by inflating at the actuarial value of 6.25 percent.
- The required accrual payments are computed for retirement pay (using 31.5 percent) and for TFL benefits (inflating the current per capita charge of $5,436 at 6.25 percent for the correct number of YOS).
- The initial level of retirement benefits at YOS 20 is computed using the High-3 formula, and annual retirement benefits for the remainder of the retiree's life span are projected out to the expected average age of death for a retiree who left the service at 20 YOS.

- The following are discounted using the standard 6 percent rate: (1) all future RMC over 20 YOS to the present, (2) retirement and health accrual amounts, also over 20 YOS, (3) future retirement benefits from age 82 for officers and 78 for enlisted pereonnel to the present by the appropriate years, and (4) future TFL health benefits from retirement to expected death.
- The final calculation is to compute the sum of all these costs to the FG and to DoD.

For the FG, the costs are the present value of RMC plus the present values of the retirement and health benefits. Note that accrual is not counted as a cost to the government, because accrual is a transfer payment from one federal agency to another. From which part of the federal budget the benefits are funded is irrelevant from a cost perspective, as we have pointed out above. We are only interested in the costs of the benefits, which are represented by the discounted values for future retirement and TFL benefits. The results? A newly commissioned officer in 2004 will cost $1,280,158 in RMC; $365,558 in retirement benefits; and $108,814 in TFL benefits, for a total lifecycle cost of $1,754,530 measured in 2004 dollars. The corresponding values for an entering member of the enlisted force who will stay to YOS 20 are somewhat less: RMC is $549,953; retirement benefits are $215,177; and TFL benefits are $102,703; for a total cost to the FG of $867,833.

Computing how much the FG could pay a civilian for the same commitment in 2004 dollars requires few facts about the civilian retirement system. The current system, the Federal Employee Retirement System (FERS), provides two different retirement benefits (note that we have not included Social Security as a benefit for either civilian or military personnel, even though both are eligible to receive it). The first is called the Basic Benefit, and it provides a retirement paycheck equal to 1 percent of the High-3 earnings multiplied by the years of creditable service, with the additional requirement that this benefit is not available until after 30 years of creditable service or age 55, whichever is higher. Unlike military retirees, civil service retirees do not receive full compensation for inflation but only CPI minus one (i.e., one percentage point less than the CPI). Obviously, this is a defined benefit plan, although considerably less generous than the military's retirement plan. The second element of FERS is the Thrift Savings Plan (TFP), which is a defined contribution plan. An employee can contribute up to 3 percent of his or her salary, with a 100 percent matching FG contribution and an additional 2 percent with a 50 percent matching contribution.[1]

With this information, the costs to the FG of hiring a new civilian employee can be computed. It is assumed that this individual will remain in federal service for 30 years, rather than the 20 YOS assumed in the military calculations, in order to compare the full costs of the retirement systems in the two cases. As before, pay growth is assumed at 3.75 percent, inflation at 3 percent, and the discount rate at 6 percent. With these assumptions, the FG can afford to pay a civilian an initial salary of $75,000 for a replaced military officer and $38,000 for a replaced enlisted person in order to break even on the civilianization. According to the federal pay schedule in 2004, this corresponded to a GS-14, step 1 for officers, and a GS-8, step 5 for enlisted personnel, not including locality pay adjustments. Since GS-14 nominally corresponds to O-5 and GS-8 to E-8, these are rather extraordinary results. They imply that the FG could replace an entry level officer with the equivalent of a lieutenant colonel or a commander, keep raising that person's pay by 3.75 percent per year for 30 years, pay retirement benefits for the remainder of that person's life, and in the end have paid out no more than it would have cost to hire an O-1 (a second lieutenant or an ensign) who would get promoted to lieutenant colonel or commander over 20 YOS and receive all of the retirement benefits to which he or she would be entitled after such service. Following the same reasoning, every single newly hired enlisted person who would rise from E-1 to an expected level of E-7 upon retirement after 20 YOS could be replaced with the equivalent of an E-8 at entry level, kept at that level

---

[1] Individuals can contribute up to 10 percent of their income to the TFP, but the final 5 percent are not matched by the FG. The additional 5 percent does receive favorable tax treatment (in that they are not taxed until withdrawal) and earn interest on deferred taxes in the meantime. We have not included the present value of this tax advantage, as it cannot be easily calculated.

with standard pay growth for 30 years, and the total costs would be the same.[2]

This makes a very strong argument for civilianization. If military career positions—officer or enlisted—can be successfully filled by federal civilians with career trajectories that begin at the usual levels and progress to retirement after 30 years, very significant federal budget outlays could be accomplished. By implication, the more military functions turned over to civilians, the greater the total savings, and this is how civilianization should be pursued: by functions and organizations and not at the individual level, searching job by job for possible swap outs. At this level, using estimates of the entire life-cycle stream of compensation and benefits under various alternatives, significant personnel savings can be achieved (naturally subject to overall strategic DoD goals, which are operational as well as fiscal and must be considered jointly). However, a defense organization that does not strategically pursue cost-efficiency is continuously sacrificing operational effectiveness, because for the same budget it could increase its capacity to support the national defense objectives. Efficiency does not mean a sacrifice of capability; the truth is quite the opposite.

How, then, would the same simple computations be performed when considering only DoD budgetary outlays? DoD is part of the FG, but that does not mean that budgetary practices necessarily lead to the same cost calculus. This can immediately be seen by the cost categories we listed above: basic pay and allowances for military personnel are the same cost items in the DoD and FG budgets, but the rest of the factors are not. We have already noted that accrual costs are not a federal cost but a federal transfer; the only relevant costs to the FG are the outlays on benefits for which accrual payments are collected. On the other hand, benefit payments are not a DoD budget cost; all out-

[2] Since these simple computations are made for illustrative purposes only, they are based on the maximum savings attainable. We have made a comparison between a military person whom we know, at entry level, will stay until vesting in the military retirement system. Obviously, the savings from civilianizations would be considerably lower if we were to compare them with military personnel who would never reach retirement; for example, by civilianizing a career that never reaches retirement and replacing it with a civilian who will reach retirement, net costs would go up, not down.

lays from federal trust funds encumber the budget of the Department of the Treasury and not the individual agencies on whose behalf the funds are held in trust. This means that the same officer whose total lifetime cost to the FG is $1,754,530 would only cost DoD the sum of RMC and retirement accrual, which for an officer is $1,568,222, or only 89.4 percent of the total federal cost. For an enlisted person, the corresponding numbers are $867,833 for the FG versus $703,189 for DoD, so that DoD's cost is only 81 percent of the total FG cost.[3]

Trust Fund Accrual Versus Cost Accounting

As these comparisons of costs between the total FG budgetary outlays and those of the DoD indicate, using accrual charges as indicators of true economic costs can be very misleading. The current accrual system in DoD does not only covers the total cost of the postretirement benefits of military personnel but also skews the cost comparison of personnel by grade or cohort, as demonstrated and discussed in Chapters Two, Three, and Four. Is there is a reason to question the very basis for this approach? Fortunately, we are not the first to address this question, and it has been forcefully answered in the context of defined benefit plans in the private sector. This has led to both a debate and a significant point of disagreement between the private Financial Accounting Standards Board (FASB) and the Federal Accounting Standards Advisory Board (FASAB).

By law, DoD actuaries use the AEAN method explained in Chapter Four. This method (1) computes the projected liability for an entering cohort and then (2) spreads that cost over all cohorts (i.e., over the entire payroll, either as a level percentage charge or as a level charge per employed person). This is called the normal cost—the ratio of the

[3] Note that we are not including the cost of TFL accrual as a cost to DoD. The reason is that, beginning in FY 2007, the Department of the Treasury will be obligated to budget for the accrual payments into the trust fund. Congress moved the funding responsibility in the 2004 National Defense Authorizations Act. If we were to consider TFL accrual payments as a DoD responsibility, the percentages of total funding for which DoD would be budgeting would be 95.7 percent for an officer and 93.8 percent for an enlisted person.

projected liability to the payroll or to the workforce. There is some controversy surrounding the use of AEAN, which is part of a family called "cost approaches." In rejecting the cost approach as an appropriate methodology, FASB stated:

> Under the cost approaches the amount attributed to a period is not the actuarial present value of a benefit earned in the period. Instead, the total cost of all the expected benefits is discounted and assigned to periods in a single mathematical step so that the net pension cost (the service cost, plus interest cost, less anticipated return on assets in the fun and to be added in future periods) is a constant amount or a constant percent of salary. . . . Under the cost approaches, the cost charged in the early years of an employee's service will provide an amount of benefit at retirement much greater than the benefits earned in those years based on the plan formula. In the last years of an employee's service, the cost is less than the present value of benefits earned. *The result is that at any point before retirement, the amount accrued for an individual under a cost approach will exceed the present value of benefits earned to that point based on the plan's benefit formula.*[4]

This is exactly what the DoD actuaries' AEAN approach does: By computing a level charge on payroll or per head, the method assigns the same cost to (1) an entry-level enlisted person who has no intention whatsoever of making a career in the military, (2) a person with 19 years of service who would never consider leaving before earning a full entitlement at 20 years, and (3) a person with 21 years of service who has already earned a full entitlement to postretirement benefits. In other words, the amounts accrued under the AEAN approach are not related to the benefits earned by various cohort members. Therefore, as argued throughout this book, AEAN does not provide an adequate measure of the cost to DoD of each person-year. As a remedy, FASB advocates methods that come from the family of "benefit approaches":

---

[4] Financial Accounting Standards Board, *Statement of Financial Accounting Standard No. 87: Employers' Accounting for Pensions*, Norwalk, Conn.: Financial Accounting Standards Board of the Financial Accounting Foundation, December 1985, para. 132 and 133, italics added.

> FASB Concepts Statement No. 3, *Elements of Financial Statements of Business Enterprises*, defines liabilities in terms of obligations, and an employer's obligation under a defined benefit plan as of a particular date is for pension benefits promised by the terms of the plan rather than for an accumulation of level costs. The Board believes that, although the "level percentage of compensation" pattern may be desirable for funding or budgeting contributions, it does not necessarily reflect how cost is incurred or how a liability arises. . . . The benefit approach adopted by the Board uses the terms of the plan to determine the benefits earned during a period (that is, the future cash flow) and then calculates the actuarial present value of those benefits. . . . In the Board's view, the benefit approaches reflect the promise of a defined benefit, and the present value of a dollar of benefit promised to a 60-year-old is greater than that of a dollar of benefit promised to a 25-year-old, if both are payable at age 65.[5]

Both the cost approach and the benefit approach yield adequately funded pension funds, as the FASB notes in this quote. And FASB did not reject the cost methods as inappropriate from a total funding perspective. However, since FASB's fundamental presumption was that postretirement benefits are contractual in nature, representing deferred compensation for present services, the terms of the plan's benefit formula should be the basis for computing the employer's liabilities. That is to say, benefits are to be discounted by expected years of service for each cohort and adjusted for the probability of reaching retirement eligibility. For these reasons, FASB advocated the use of various formulas from a family called the "unit credit" approaches, where the employer's liability each year is equal to the earned benefits under the plan. For plans with cliff vesting, this requires spreading the liability over service years in proportion to the likelihood of attaining vesting.[6]

---

5 FASB, *Statement of Financial Accounting Standard No. 87*, para. 131, 132, 133.

6 The approach we have adopted throughout this study of spreading retirement costs according to retirement probabilities is consistent with a benefit approach, although not necessarily constituting a full-blown version of a complete actuarial funding method, as we have not attempted to reconstitute a trust fund process consistent with our method of estimating the costs of a military person-year.

However, the view that cost approaches like AEAN are inappropriate for defined benefit plans has not been accepted by the FG. Here is the response from the FASAB, which has been approved by OMB, the Department of the Treasury, and GAO:

> The major federal pension plans use an actuarial cost method for funding purposes known as aggregate entry age normal (AEAN). Various actuarial cost methods exist. All the methods regarded as acceptable methods for advance funding of private pension plans recognize the cost of employee's pension benefits during the employee's years of service, but the different actuarial methods recognize the cost in different patterns over time. The AEAN method is intended to produce a periodic pension cost that is a level percent of payroll. . . . FASAB concluded that any method of assigning the value of benefits that are earned over the entire career to particular years of service involves a process of estimation. It is, of course, reasonable to assume that the benefits accrue in some sort of systematic and uniform fashion and not, for example, all at once when the employee becomes eligible. Assuming that the benefits accrue as a uniform percentage of salary each year (as is done with AEAN for pensions) is a reasonable approach. AEAN is particularly useful within an organization when measuring costs over time because it provides that a dollar of salary always equals a fixed percent of pension, regardless of the year involved. . . . FASAB specified the AEAN for several reasons. First, as stated, AEAN is a reasonable and systematic way of allocating costs evenly over the service lives of employees. Second, the major federal retirement systems [the Military Retirement System (MRS), the Civil Service Retirement System (CSRS) and the Federal Employees Retirement System (FERS)] use AEAN . . . . [7]

Boiled down to its essentials, this statement says that AEAN represents the manner in which benefits are earned and that it should be

---

[7] Office of Management and Budget, *Accounting for Liabilities of the Federal Government*, Federal Financial Accounting Standard No. 5, Executive Office of the President, Washington, D.C., September 1995, pp. 149–152.

used because it is being used. Ignoring the last point, one may note that the first part of the argument is factually incorrect: The military retirement system is singular in its cliff vesting of benefits. Under the benefit rules of the plan, as established by law, there are no benefits for persons leaving prior to 20 YOS and only small increments to those who stay beyond. It is an extreme system under which the majority of people who enter the military will earn no benefits whatsoever. It is simply factually incorrect to state that benefits are earned in proportion to salaries, when the majority of employees who are regularly assessed normal cost accrual charges will never earn any benefits whatsoever. Perhaps in recognition of this awkward fact, FASAB is not as unyielding as one might think:

> The Board recognizes that some analysts might, for some purposes, want to consider an alternative measure of compensation costs, e.g., one that includes interest on the part of the pension (or ORB [other retirement benefits]) liability that relates to current workers, or one that recognizes some non-service costs over the workers' years of expected service. Special analysis and reports will always be necessary for special purposes. General purpose financial reports must, by definition, focus on the most common needs of users of those reports.[8]

In other words, if there are reasons to display the costs of the retirement system in a different manner, OMB and FASAB do not reject such approaches out of hand. If a good case can be made, alternative methods of accounting for postretirement benefits can be used as a particular situation demands. Therefore, the analytical approaches outlined in this study may, in principle, be used as the foundation for special analyses when appropriate. However, FASAB rejects the notion that AEAN is inappropriate for defined benefit plans in the public sector.

The only substantive difference between the cost approach and the benefit approach is in how they spread a total employer liability

---

[8] Office of Management and Budget, *Accounting for Liabilities of the Federal Government*, p. 163.

over the service years of the employees. The cost approach favors a simple percent of payroll or level charge per person, and this has obvious advantages from a budgeting perspective, which is one important reason that it is favored by OMB and federal actuaries. In their view, overall budget accountability is the primary criterion for financial integrity, and AEAN methods provide that accountability and are technically easy to compute. However, lost in this approach is the ability to attribute the cost of postretirement benefits to individual work-years, as all work-years cost the same when the total cost is spread in a level manner across all service years. The benefits of simplicity and visibility come at the price of a proper estimate of the cost of pension benefits attributable to each service year. As we have repeatedly demonstrated above, the AEAN method yields incorrect conclusions if used to assess the cost to the FG of an individual military person-year. In defense of federal actuaries, it must be noted that the AEAN method was never intended to be used for this purpose; its explicit purpose is to ensure adequate funding for total FG pension liabilities, which it accomplishes without fault. However, the AEAN approach must be discarded in attempts to estimate the cost of individual military person-years. And this does not yet provide an answer as to how the gains and losses from managerial actions should be allocated among responsible agency decisionmakers.

FASB views plan assets as owned by the employer, so that any actuarial gains/losses to such assets accrue to the employer. This is at the very heart of the benefit approach, under which each year an employer computes any changes in pension benefits earned by employees that year. This includes all employees, not just the entry cohort. Thus, if it should happen that an unexpected exodus of personnel prior to vesting creates an actuarial gain in the assets of the defined benefit plan, this gain accrues immediately to the employer and will be used to compute the firm's liability for the next year. Under this approach, the employer immediately realizes any financial gains from improved efficiencies. FASB's preference for the benefit approaches is based on the argument that the benefit approach provides a more appropriate assessment of the firm's overall financial status than the cost approach, and the information it generates is therefore of greater importance to creditors and investors.

FASAB does not take that position. Instead, FASAB makes a distinction between the employing entity (such as the federal agency in charge of hiring and personnel management) and the administrative entity (the FG, responsible for paying salaries and benefits). FASAB is of the opinion that all gains/losses should be accounted for by the administrative entity, not the employing entity. This is the essence of the cost approach: AEAN assesses the pension costs of each entry cohort and spreads the normal cost over all present service years in the force. Should the employing entity (in this case DoD) significantly reduce some cohorts in the workforce prior to its members becoming vested, this will not in any way change the accrual costs under the AEAN method by virtue of actuarial gain to the trust fund from past accrual that now will not be used for future benefit payments. AEAN looks only at the entry cohort and only looks forward, as indicated by its method of computing the ratio of expected benefits to expected service years.[9] By practice, the DoD boards of actuaries deal with unfunded liabilities in two different ways: (1) unfunded liabilities arising from new entitlements to non-entry cohorts are assigned to the Department of the Treasury, and (2) actuarial gains/losses arising from changing or unrealized assumptions are charged to DoD by altering the normal cost. Under this procedure, a drawdown of military personnel sufficient to cause a significant actuarial gain would assign that gain to the Department of the Treasury in the form of reduced future outlays from the trust funds. If a civilianization action were to save significantly on postretirement benefits, current actuarial procedures would not allow DoD to capture these gains as a result of its attempts to gain efficiencies through civilianization.

Obviously, unlike a private employer, DoD does own the assets in the pension fund. Nominally, both the military retirement and the

[9] If the actuaries were to use the same description of conventional force management principles explained by Robbert and Gates, then transition probabilities for the smaller cohorts would not change and the AEAN accrual percentage (the normal cost) would remain the same. This means that only total contributions change under the AEAN method, not the per-person accrual.

TFL trust funds are managed by the Department of the Treasury. But where are their assets? The Social Security Trust Fund can help provide an answer to this question, since all federal trust funds are managed according to the same principles and much more attention has been focused on Social Security than on military retirement. Where are the assets of the Social Security Trust Fund? The Social Security Administration provides the following questions and answers regarding the future of its assets:

> Q. Does Social Security have dedicated assets invested for my retirement?
>
> A. Social Security is largely a "pay-as-you-go" system with today's taxpayers paying for the benefits of today's retirees. Money not needed to pay today's benefits is invested in special-issue Treasury bonds.
>
> Q. Is there really a Social Security trust fund?
>
> A. Yes. Presently, Social Security collects more in taxes than it pays in benefits. The excess is borrowed by the U.S. Treasury, which in turn issues special-issue Treasury bonds to Social Security. These bonds totaled $1.7 trillion at the beginning of 2005. Social Security received $89 billion in interest from bonds in 2004. However, Social Security is still basically a "pay-as-you-go" system as the $1.7 trillion is a small percent of benefit obligations. [10]

The point of these answers is that there is a small trust fund, representing the excess of today's collections and interest income over current outlays. But since the assets held this way are a small proportion of benefit obligations, the answer suggests that Social Security is really a pay-as-you-go system. This is, at best, a misleading answer, because the trust fund's assets have been converted to treasury bonds, which in turn have been used to finance the current deficit federal tax revenues in relation to federal spending. Therefore, the "assets" in the trust fund are really claims on future tax revenues. Under current projections, the

[10] U.S. Social Security Administration, "Social Security's Future—FAQs," Web page, January 12, 2007.

revenues for Social Security will be insufficient to pay current benefits after the year 2041, and then the "assets" in the trust fund will have to be reclaimed (i.e., the treasury bonds will have to be sold and converted to cash for benefit payments). There are only two ways for the FG to manage this: by raising taxes to redeem the bonds or by borrowing new money by issuing new treasury bonds putting that money in the Social Security Trust Fund to be used for benefit payments. The real point here is that the "assets" in the trust fund, having been already spent on current consumption, only represent a claim on future taxpayers. It is irrelevant whether the Social Security Trust Fund has any nominal assets at all.[11] If it does, they are spent and converted to liabilities for current or future taxpayers; if it does not, all benefit payments are funded by current taxes. Either way, Social Security is a pay-as-you-go system having only paper assets—and the word of the FG—to back it up.[12]

---

[11] Since all current government bonds are implicit liabilities of future taxpayers, there has long been a sophisticated discussion among economists about whether treasury bonds should ever be counted as wealth, even when held by private investors. The basic idea is called "Ricardian equivalence," the essence of which is that tax financing and deficit financing of current government expenditures have identical effects on the economy, and that the intertemporal difference in the timing of taxation between the two financing systems is irrelevant. Raising future taxes reduces current wealth in exactly the same way that current taxes reduce current wealth. Under this argument, government bonds only represent future taxpayer liabilities, no matter whether held by a federal trust fund or by private individuals, and should never be counted as net social assets. The technical literature is admirably reviewed and summarized by John Seater, who concludes that the Ricardian equivalence argument holds up well under the best econometric tests (John Seater, "Ricardian Equivalence," *Journal of Economic Literature*, Vol. 31, No. 1, March 1993, pp. 142–190), and Roger Kormendi and Aris Protopapadakis provide a recent update confirming Seater's findings (Roger Kormendi and Aris Protopapadakis, "Budget Deficits, Real Yields, and Current Account Deficits: The Systematic Evidence on Ricardian Equivalence," unpublished working paper, October 2005, available on request from the authors at kormendi@kgpartners.com or aris.protopapadakis@marshall.usc.edu, cited with permission).

[12] Professional economists have always recognized that Social Security is a pay-as-you-go system. For a good example, see Alan D. Viard, "Pay-As-You-Go Social Security and the Aging of America," *Federal Reserve Bank of Dallas Economic and Financial Policy Review*, Vol. 1, No. 4, 2002, with many excellent references to the technical economic literature on the subject.

All of this is also true of the two trust funds holding nominal "assets" for future DoD retirees. These trust funds are, in reality, only bookkeeping devices. All benefits paid out of the trust funds are financed on a pay-as-you-go basis. Current taxpayers pay the benefits of current military retirees, and future taxpayers will pay the benefits of future military retirees. This must be the case as long as the assets in federal trust funds are invested only in Treasury bonds; obviously, if federal trust fund assets were invested in the stocks and bonds issued by privately held corporations, the story would be a different. However, the important conclusion to reach from this discussion of federal trust funds is that if DoD realizes important savings in retirement benefits through civilianizing military careers, the only beneficiaries of that are future taxpayers, at least under the current rules.

Thus, there are two critical issues arising from the use of the AEAN method to estimate the costs of a military person-year in the context of a civilianization action. The first is that AEAN was never intended to provide the correct cost of a service year, only to ensure adequate funding of a defined benefit pension plan. The second is that AEAN does not allow DoD to capture any pension-related gains created by its efforts to improve military and civilian personnel management. The obvious conclusions are that AEAN must be rejected as a means of generating cost estimates and that DoD must seek the cooperation of OMB and Congress in improving financial incentives for the military services to search for savings through personnel management.

On the Equity and Efficiency of the Military Compensation System

As we have noted in several places, only a minority of an entering cohort of military personnel will ever stay to YOS 20 and vest in the retirement system. Obviously, two implications can be drawn form this fact. One is that, although two persons in the same cohort may have served together for a dozen or more years and have exactly the same experience and ability, if one of them stays to retirement and the other does not, their cost to the government (and the total pay and benefits that they receive from the FG throughout their lifetimes) is very different. This raises the issue of fairness (i.e., is it equitable to allow such differences in pay for the same job in a public corporation?). The second implication is that the non-career force is clearly much cheaper for the FG than the career force, which raises an issue of efficiency (i.e., are there practical ways of reducing the career content of the present military services, in order to realize significant savings in postretirement benefits?). We do not propose to answer these questions definitively here, but offer them for potential consideration in future debates and discussions of the military pay system.

If we confine attention to the DoD costs and ignore the difference between the costs to the FG and to DoD, we can use the approach developed in Chapter Three in which we spread the DoD actuaries' accrual across service years in proportion to the likelihood of reaching retirement eligibility. Since the percentage of each year-group that is statistically likely to retire is known, compensation can be divided between those who will retire and those who will not. Figure 6.1 and Figure 6.2 show the results of this computation for officers and enlisted personnel, respectively.

On average, military personnel who do not stay in the service long enough to reach retirement eligibility earn between 60 and 70 percent of the compensation of similarly qualified personnel who do stay to retirement eligibility. As suggested, it is possible to think of this as an issue of equity. While a common counter to this argument is that as individuals entering the force are all treated the same and have exactly the same chances of staying to YOS 20, there is no question of fairness or equity arising from the disparity in pay—military personnel understand the differences in rules that apply to careerists and non-careerists. This argument is, of course, valid up to a point. Still, the history of military compensation is rife with references to unfairness and inequity across services and grades, usually raised in the context of an effort to increase in compensation for one group or another. It is interesting to note that the concept of equal pay for equal performance receives such short shrift in discussions of the retirement compensation system.

Figure 6.1
Comparison of Compensation to Likely Retirees and Nonretirees, Enlisted Personnel

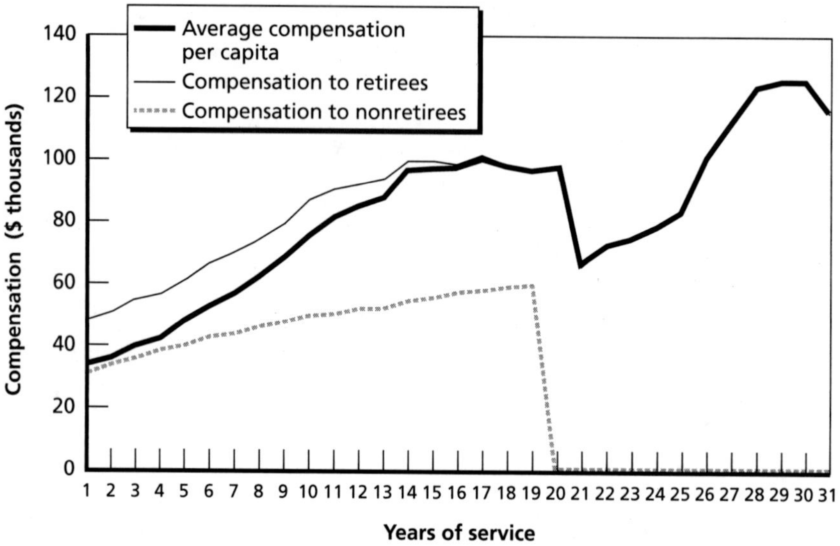

RAND *MG598-6.1*

Using the same methodology, it is possible to also divide up the entire DoD military personnel between those who will retire and those who will not, as shown in Figure 6.3.

The chart on the left indicates that at any point in time, 51.6 percent of individual in the force are likely to reach retirement eligibility, and the remaining 48.4 percent are not.[13] The chart on the right shows that likely retirees receive 70 percent of the total compensation paid out by DoD; the non-retirees receive less than 30 percent. This is an inevitable outcome of the cliff-vesting rule that requires a full 20 YOS before any retirement benefits accrue, along with very generous postretirement benefits; it means that those who for whatever reason do not complete YOS 20 receive less compensation for the same work.

---

[13] We have noted how the majority of DoD personnel will not reach retirement eligibility. This is true for the entering cohorts, and it is also true if the denominator includes all those who at one point were in the service but have since left. In the Figure 6.2, the denominator comprises only personnel in uniform.

Figure 6.2
Comparison of Compensation to Likely Retirees and Nonretirees, Officers

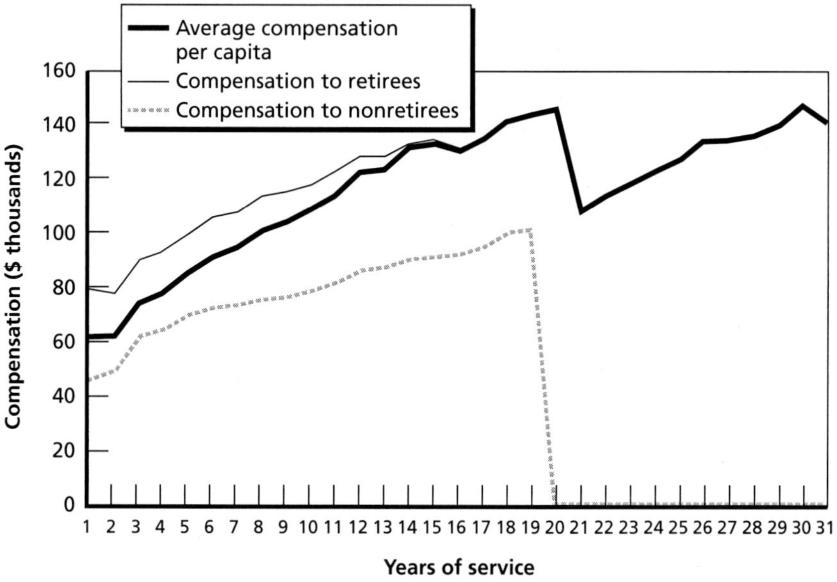

RAND *MG598-6.2*

Figure 6.3
Retirees and Nonretirees, Population and Compensation

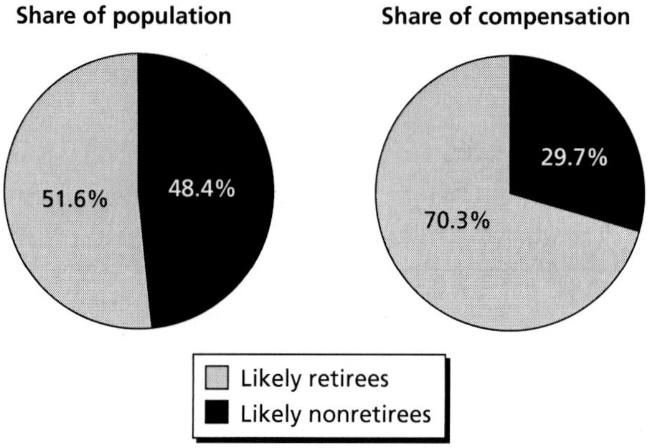

RAND *MG598-6.3*

We leave for others to argue whether or not this is a compelling reason to revamp the current military retirement system.

These equity considerations may be dismissed as irrelevant, but the arguments just made do have efficiency implications. Since the noncareer force is so much cheaper to the FG, careful cost management would seem to suggest maximizing the use of noncareerists.[14] This is a question of force shape: Should the force be heavy with careerists, or should the services move toward a forced comprised mostly of short-term, rapid-turnover personnel? Usually, the analyses of these issues revolve around the value of experience and the cost of training, with the implication that the easier the tasks and the training, the younger the force in those career fields can be. Or, as in the case of the Marine Corps, a military service may value youth, vigor, and physical strength in its enlisted force and for these reasons keep its career force as small as possible. To these arguments, we only wish to add that cost considerations also matter, and that they have implications for force shaping that may become of importance as the need for budget stringency increases. If that should happen, the question as to how to provide a service with sufficient financial incentives to undertake the difficult career management changes that a significant alteration of the personnel pyramid would entail becomes particularly important.

Final Note

In the end, it would seem that the question of civilianization is only one of the issues that DoD should address from the perspective of the cost analyses of postretirement benefits presented in this study. Along with civilianization policies, force management and force shaping turn out to be of significant importance in managing personnel costs. In addition (and an issue that has not been pursued above), it is obvious that reserve forces have cost advantages that can also be substantial,

---

[14] Rebalancing the career/noncareer force mix may require raising current compensation offers, if entrants are attracted by the probability vesting.

since the retirement benefits of reservists are much lower than those of the active-duty forces.

Yet the most pressing issue for DoD would appear to be to begin to work with OMB and Congress to find an acceptable budgetary method for giving present personnel managers in the services adequate credit and financial incentives for reducing the costs of postretirement benefits to the FG. Those cost reductions presently accrue by necessity only to future taxpayers, by reducing the projections for future outlays of retirement benefits. Still, cost reductions for future taxpayers have value today, and DoD should find a way to ensure that current managers receive adequate incentives and rewards for making good long-term decisions, even when the benefits will accrue only after they will have left DoD.

This work has pointed out large problems with the current military retirement system, but we do not propose that it should be eliminated. The current system is characterized by a number of very severe weaknesses, among which we deem the following to be the most important:

- It militates against effective force management and inventory shaping.
- It is unfair to those who may work for up to 20 years and not see any benefits.
- It is costly and inefficient in that it does not correspond with the empirical high personal discount rates among military personnel, which implies that they would prefer more current compensation and less retirement pay (leading to a much less costly compensation system for the same force).
- It is fundamentally imbalanced and unsustainable combination of cash and health benefits, with the latter growing at such a rapid rate that the two combined will outstrip the total current value of retirement benefits in a few decades.[15]

---

[15] We have two bases for making this statement. First, the very generous health benefits for military personnel offered by TFL were not based on any analysis of the effects retention behaviors and were objected to by DoD when Congress first proposed them. Thus, there was no indication that these expensive benefits were required to induce lower leave rates. Second,

While a recent commission has proposed revising the military retirement system,[16] this work demonstrates that more-efficient buyout schemes can easily be financed without changing the retirement system. If the force shaping potential of the approach developed in our study were to be implemented in practice, it would also ameliorate somewhat one of the most invidious negative implications of the current, outdated military retirement system.

---

the differential growth rates of future cash benefits compared to health benefits will cause the total value of the retirement package not to rise very rapidly while greatly increasing the proportion of the total package given over to health benefits. There is much economic research that suggests that, if given a choice between cash and in-kind benefits, people generally prefer cash. For these reasons, it is very difficult to believe that military personnel at some point in the future will not demand a change in the composition of the retirement package to less health and more cash.

16 See Defense Advisory Committee on Military Compensation, *The Military Compensation System: Completing the Transition to an All-Volunteer Force*, Washington, D.C., April 2006. This issue is also being pursued by another defense study commission, the 10th Quadrennial Review of Military Compensation, which will produce a report next year pursuant to a standing congressional mandate.

APPENDIX

Grades and Titles for Military Officers and Enlisted Personnel

Table A.1
Grades and Titles for Military Officers and Enlisted Personnel

	Title by Service			
Grade	**Army**	**Marines**	**Air Force**	**Navy**
Officers				
O-10	General	General	General	Admiral
O-9	Lieutenant general	Lieutenant general	Lieutenant general	Vice admiral
O-8	Major general	Major general	Major general	Rear admiral, upper half
O-7	Brigadier general	Brigadier general	Brigadier general	Rear admiral, lower half
O-6	Colonel	Colonel	Colonel	Captain
O-5	Lieutenant colonel	Lieutenant colonel	Lieutenant colonel	Commander
O-4	Major	Major	Major	Lieutenant commander
O-3	Captain	Captain	Captain	Lieutenant
O-2	First lieutenant	First lieutenant	First lieutenant	Lieutenant, junior grade
O-1	Second lieutenant	Second lieutenant	Second lieutenant	Ensign

Table A.1—Continued

	Title by Service			
Grade	**Army**	**Marines**	**Air Force**	**Navy**
Enlisted Personnel				
E-9	Sergeant major	Sergeant major	Chief master sergeant	Master chief petty officer
E-8	Master sergeant	Master sergeant	Senior master sergeant	Senior chief petty officer
E-7	Sergeant, first class	Gunnery sergeant	Master sergeant	Chief petty officer
E-6	Staff sergeant	Staff sergeant	Technical sergeant	Petty officer, first class
E-5	Sergeant	Sergeant	Staff sergeant	Petty officer, second class
E-4	Corporal	Corporal	Senior airman	Petty officer, third class
E-3	Private, first class	Lance corporal	Airman, first class	Seaman
E-2	Private, E-2	Private, first class	Airman	Seaman apprentice
E-1	Private	Private	Basic airman	Seaman recruit

References

Defense Advisory Committee on Military Compensation, *The Military Compensation System: Completing the Transition to an All-Volunteer Force*, Washington, D.C., April 2006. As of February 28, 2007: http://www.dod.gov/prhome/docs/dacmc_finalreport7_11.pdf

Financial Accounting Standards Board, *Statement of Financial Accounting Standard No. 87: Employers' Accounting for Pensions*, Norwalk, Conn.: Financial Accounting Standards Board of the Financial Accounting Foundation, December 1985. As of February 28, 2007: www.fasb.org/pdf/fas87.pdf

Gates, Susan M., and Albert A. Robbert, *Comparing the Costs of DoD Military and Civil Service Personnel*, Santa Monica, Calif.: RAND Corporation, MR-980-OSD, 1998. As of February 28, 2007: www.rand.org/pubs/monograph_reports/MR980/

Hix, William M., and William W. Taylor, *A Policymaker's Guide to Accrual Funding of Military Retirement*, Santa Monica, Calif.: RAND Corporation, MR-760-A, 1997. As of February 28, 2007: http://www.rand.org/pubs/monograph_reports/MR760/

Kormendi, Roger, and Aris Protopapadakis, "Budget Deficits, Real Yields, and Current Account Deficits: The Systematic Evidence on Ricardian Equivalence," unpublished working paper, October 2005. Available upon request from the authors at kormendi@kgpartners.com or aris.protopapadakis@marshall.usc.edu and cited in this work with their permission.

Military.com, "TRICARE for Life," Web page, n.d. As of February 28, 2007: http://www.military.com/benefits/tricare/tricare-for-life/tricare-for-life-and-dual-eligibility

Office of Management and Budget, *Accounting for Liabilities of the Federal Government*, Federal Financial Accounting Standard No. 5, Executive Office of the President, Washington, D.C., September 1995. As of February 28, 2007: http://www.fasab.gov/pdffiles/sffas-5.pdf

Palmer, Adele R., and David J. Osbaldeston, *Incremental Costs of Military and Civilian Manpower in the Military Services*, Santa Monica, Calif.: RAND Corporation, N-2677-FMP, 1988. As of February 28, 2007:
http://www.rand.org/pubs/notes/N2677/

Public Law 106-398, *The Floyd D. Spence National Defense Authorizations Act for FY 2001*, Section 713, Chapter 56.

Public Law 108-375, *The Ronald W. Reagan National Defense Authorization Act for 2005*, Section 725.

Schoenbaum, Michael, Barbara O. Wynn, Terri Tanielian, Katherine M. Harris, Renee Labor, and C. Ross Anthony, *Health Benefits for Medicare Eligible Military Retirees: Rationalizing TRICARE for Life*, Santa Monica, Calif.: RAND Corporation, TR-118-OSD, 2004. As of February 28, 2007:
http://www.rand.org/pubs/technical_reports/TR118/

Seater, John, "Ricardian Equivalence," *Journal of Economic Literature*, Vol. 31, No. 1, March 1993, pp. 142–190.

United States Code, Title 10, Chapter 74, "Military Retirement Trust Fund," January 3, 2005.

———, Title 37, Section 101(25), January 3, 2005.

U.S. Department of Defense, "Guidance for Manpower Management," Department of Defense Directive 1100.4, February 12, 2005. As of February 28, 2007:
http://www.dtic.mil/whs/directives/corres/html/110004.htm

———, "Guidance for Determining Workforce Mix," Department of Defense Directive 1100.22, September 7, 2006. As of February 28, 2007:
http://www.dtic.mil/whs/directives/corres/html/110022.htm

U.S. Department of Defense, Civilian Personnel Management System, "National Personnel Management System," Web site, February 1, 2007. As of February 28, 2007:
http://www.cpms.osd.mil/nsps/

U.S. Department of Defense, Office of the Actuary, *Valuation of the Military Retirement System*, Arlington, Va., September 30, 2004. As of February 28, 2007:
http://www.dod.mil/actuary/valbook2004a.pdf

U.S. Department of Defense, Office of the Assistant Secretary of Defense (Health Affairs), and the TRICARE Management Activity, "TRICARE for Life," Web site, October 12, 2006. As of February 28, 2007:
http://www.tricare.mil/tfl/default.cfm

U.S. Department of Defense, Office of the Under Secretary of Defense (Comptroller), "Military Composite Standard Pay and Reimbursement Rates, Fiscal Year 2005," September 16, 2004. As of February 28, 2007:
http://www.dod.mil/comptroller/rates/fy2005/2005_k.pdf

U.S. Department of Defense, Office of the Under Secretary for Personnel and Readiness, Directorate of Compensation, *Selected Military Compensation Tables*, also known as the *Green Book*, January 1, 2006.

U.S. Government Accountability Office, *Military Personnel: DoD Needs to Improve the Transparency and Reassess the Reasonableness, Appropriateness, Affordability, and Sustainability of Its Military Compensation System*, Washington, D.C., GAO-05-798, July 2005. As of February 28, 2007:
http://www.gao.gov/new.items/d05798.pdf

U.S. Social Security Administration, "Social Security's Future—FAQs," Web page, January 12, 2007. As of February 28, 2007:
http://www.ssa.gov/qa.htm

Viard, Alan D., "Pay-As-You-Go Social Security and the Aging of America," *Federal Reserve Bank of Dallas Economic and Financial Policy Review*, Vol. 1, No. 4, 2002. As of February 28, 2007:
http://dallasfedreview.org/pdfs/v01_n04_a01.pdf

Warner, John T., and Saul Pleeter, "The Personal Discount Rate: Evidence from Military Downsizing Programs," *American Economic Review*, Vol. 91, No.1, March 2001, pp. 33–53.